Slam Dunk Cover Letters

Slam Dunk Cover Letters

Second Edition

MARK ROWH

McGraw-Hill
New York   Chicago   San Francisco
Lisbon   London   Madrid   Mexico City   Milan
Montreal   New Delhi   San Juan   Seoul   Singapore
Sydney   Toronto

1 2 3 4 5 6 7 8 9 0   QPD/QPD   0 9 8 7 6 5

ISBN 0-07-143901-3

This publication is designed to provide accurate and authoritative information in regard to the subject matter covered. It is sold with the understanding that neither the author nor the publisher is engaged in rendering legal, accounting, or other professional service. If legal advice or other expert assistance is required, the services of a competent professional person should be sought.
—From a Declaration of Principles jointly adopted by Committee of the American Bar Association and a Committee of Publishers.

McGraw-Hill books are available at special quantity discounts to use as premiums and sales promotions, or for use in corporate training programs. For more information, please write to the Director of Special Sales, McGraw-Hill Professional, Two Penn Plaza, New York, NY 10121-2298. Or contact your local bookstore.

Library of Congress Cataloging-in-Publication Data

Rowh, Mark.
 Slam dunk cover letters / by Mark Rowh.—2nd ed.
   p. cm.
  ISBN 0-07-143901-3 (alk. paper)
  1. Cover letters. 2. Applications for positions. I. Title
HF5383.R68 2005
650.14'2—dc22

2004022403

This book is dedicated to

my friends across the Atlantic,

the Daltons: Basil,

Margaret, Amy, Lucy and Niall.

Contents

1 **Slam Dunk Cover Letters**   *1*

2 **Cover Letter Fundamentals**   *5*

3 **Two Basic Styles of Cover Letters**   *15*

4 **Playing the Cover Letter Game**   *69*

5 **Using Cover Letters to Best Advantage**   *83*

6 **More Sample Slam Dunk Cover Letters**   *87*

Appendix A: Helpful Resources   *119*

Appendix B: Helpful Words and Phrases to Use
in Cover Letters   *121*

Appendix C: Preliminary Worksheet   *123*

Appendix D: Submission Worksheet   *125*

Slam Dunk Cover Letters

1

Slam Dunk Cover Letters

In today's cutthroat business world, seeking a job might not seem like a game. But there are winners and there are losers in the job-search process, and you don't want to fall into the latter category.

One way to be a winner is to write clear, powerful cover letters. When combined with first-rate resumes (the kind described by Steven Provenzano in his dynamite book, *Slam Dunk Resumes*), well-written cover letters can help you make a great impression on a potential employer. Even in a world of Internet job sites and e-mail communications (more on that later), cover letters or their equivalents play an important role in the job search process.

First impressions count. This might be a cliché, but it's true nevertheless. The initial impression you make on an employer sets the stage for everything that comes later. And in many situations, the first thing an employer sees is the letter you use to accompany a resume or job application.

Just think about this for a minute. Picture a busy manager, juggling meetings, phone calls, and other responsibilities. On her desk is a pile of resumes along with other letters, memos, and documents. Among them is your letter of application and accompanying resume—precious to you, but just one of many that this manager will see today.

Will your letter make a good impression? Will it cause this employer to want to learn more about you by reading the resume, and perhaps even inviting you for an interview? If so, your letter has served its purpose.

On the other hand, what if your letter is mediocre or worse? Keep in mind that in looking through a stack of applications, the first move of some employers is not to pull out the single most promising letter or resume. Most take a different approach. They glance through the applications, and then summarily weed out those that do not seem a good match for the position. In other words, employers might be looking for reasons to disregard your application, especially in highly competitive situations where the number of applicants far exceeds the number of job openings. This might sound negative, but it's one of the realities of the hiring process. So what do you do? The most important step is to make sure your letter does not cause you to be disregarded. At a minimum, it should be clear and error free.

Of course, the opposite approach also has merit. Instead of merely avoiding major flaws, you think in more positive terms. This means taking pains to make your letter stand out from others because it is so good.

THE JOB APPLICANT'S APPROACH TO WRITING

When you consider the phrase *applying for a job*, you might first think of resumes, application forms, interviews, and other trappings of the job application process.

If you've spent a great deal of time preparing a resume, you might not have put much thought into developing effective cover letters. But the truth is, cover letters can be essential to your success. As mentioned before, in many cases your cover letter is the first point of contact between you and the person who makes the hiring decisions.

Job applicants, like others who already hold established positions, must follow standard practices expected of any written communication between literate people. At the same time, you often face an extra challenge: grabbing the attention of the recipient while making a positive impression. You must make your case as a promising job candidate—all within the confines of a brief piece of correspondence.

Application letters may be read by many types of people. Certainly, human resources professionals constitute a primary audience. But other possible readers include clerical staff, supervisors, executive managers, members of departments where job openings occur, and consultants assisting in the hiring process.

To enhance your chances of landing any job, you must be able to communicate with each of these audiences. In writing for them, you'll want to make sure every letter has certain basic features. Like other correspondence, a cover letter should offer these qualities:

- It should be clear and understandable.
- It should focus on the specifics of why you are corresponding (for example, the particular job in which you are interested).
- It should feature an attractive appearance while conforming to commonly accepted standards of business communication.

Kevin Donlin, president of Guaranteed Resumes, an international resume and job search firm, makes an interesting point about the importance of cover letters in today's ultracompetitive hiring environment.

Some employers place a lot of emphasis on the cover letter and some don't. That means you must err on the side of including a cover letter. For some, the cover letter can knock out a marginal candidate if it's poorly written or sloppy, so it must look professional.

He also points out that a well-written cover letter is crucial for anyone making a career transition. "The cover letter should make it clear that the writer has the right skills and experience for the job, even if that person is coming from another industry," he says.

The Why/What Test

Before beginning the letter-writing process, apply the why/what test. Ask yourself these questions:

1. Why am I taking the trouble to write this?
2. Why would anyone want or need to read it?
3. What do I want to achieve?
4. What reaction is it likely to provoke in the reader?

By answering these why/what questions, you will establish the framework for your letter-writing efforts.

GO AHEAD—WRITE IN THIS BOOK!

This book is intended as a helpful, practical resource, not a volume to be stuck on a shelf. Feel free (unless this is a library copy) to do any or all of the following:

- Underline key passages.
- Write in the margins.
- Fill out the Preliminary Worksheet.
- Make photocopies of the Submission Worksheet, and fill out one for each job for which you apply.
- Tear out sample letters, mark them up, and use them in developing your own versions.

Remember, only the finished product must look neat! You can use this book for notes, rough-draft development, and more.

2
Cover Letter Fundamentals

WHY COVER LETTERS ARE IMPORTANT

Why bother with a letter at all? Can't you just send in your resume and let it stand for itself? Actually, that *might* work in some cases, but such a practice could also lead to some undesirable results. For example, if a manager received a resume in the mail without an accompanying letter, he might not realize which position you would like to pursue. Or a secretary, unaware of any openings at the time, might file the resume without passing it on to a manager. Or if an employer received five resumes but yours was the only one without a cover letter, it could appear inadequate compared to the others.

The truth is that cover letters can serve several important functions. Here are some basic reasons for taking the time to put together a cover letter.

1. **It might be required.** Some ads and job announcements specify that a letter of application must be submitted. They might also require other information, typically a resume or completed application. But if employers stipulate that a letter be submitted, there is no getting around it. After all, they're the bosses—or at least, you hope they'll become yours!

2. **It can tie a resume to a specific job opening.** A given employer might have several job openings at any one time. If you send in a resume without an identifying cover letter, it might not be obvious which job you're ap-

plying for. By specifying in a cover letter exactly which job (or job category) you'd like to be considered for, you prevent any possible confusion about your intent.

3. **It can connect a resume to a specific person.** A letter, even if it's written for business purposes, is a personal document. When it is directed to a specific person, business etiquette demands that the intended recipient actually receive this correspondence. After all, no one wants her letter filed away in some anonymous area such as the personnel department. While there are no guarantees (some managers, especially in large organizations, might delegate the task of reading and answering mail to others), a cover letter greatly increases the odds that your resume will end up where you intend it.

4. **It can bring focus to a designated time frame.** Most resumes are undated. Even if you do add a date to each new version of your resume, it might not be clear when a given resume has been submitted, especially in organizations that receive large numbers of job applications. But a dated cover letter clarifies exactly when a resume has been submitted. This might be important, especially if the employer has specified an application deadline. Some employers refuse to accept applications that fail to meet an announced deadline. Even if that is not the case, it makes good sense to include dated correspondence with any resume or other material you submit to a potential employer. In this way, you and your potential employer can avoid confusion, and (in the case of repeated applications over time), it will always be obvious which is the most recent application.

5. **It can emphasize a personal connection.** "It's not *what* you know but *who* you know." Those who believe that people should be hired solely on merit generally hate the sentiment expressed in this well-known phrase. Certainly it represents a vast oversimplification of the way employers fill job openings. But if you *do* have a personal connection to a company or one of its employees, a cover letter is a great place to mention it. We're not talking shady ethics here; it might be something as simple as having worked for a friend of your potential employer, and then pointing out that connection in a letter. If you did a good job, and the two employers are good friends, you might grab a quick advantage over the competition.

6. **It can highlight, clarify, or enhance information presented in a resume.** This is probably the most important feature of a slam dunk cover letter. Even an inferior cover letter can serve most of the functions listed above. But an excellent letter does more. It strengthens your case for employment by pointing out key information in your favor. This might be a summary of two or three important facts covered in more detail in your resume. Or it might be a fact that is not listed in the resume but is relevant to one particular employer. At any rate, with such information presented in the brief, easy-to-read format of a short letter, the employer can glance over this material and immediately obtain an idea of who you are and why you should be considered for a job.

Just *how* to present such information is explained later. But don't underestimate the potential of a carefully crafted letter to help open the doors to the job you want.

DO COVER LETTERS FIT IN THE ELECTRONIC AGE?

With the growth of e-mail and Internet job sites, using the mail to transmit cover letters is not as common as it once was. Some might even wonder if cover letters have become a dated concept. But experts agree that they still have their place.

Here's the general thinking:

- Whenever you use the time-tested approach of mailing a resume or delivering it in person, a cover letter is an absolute must.

- If you are submitting a resume by e-mail, a covering message is still a necessity. This might take the form of an e-mail message, or it might be a traditional letter formatted as an e-mail attachment. In either case, the same type of information should be included, even if the format varies somewhat.

- If a resume is posted on an Internet site, the need for a cover letter might still apply. In some cases this will mean posting the kinds of details traditionally included in a cover letter. In others, it might involve following up a response that was prompted by electronic communications with the submission of a traditional letter.

Heath Shackleford, an expert on interviewing and communications, says job applicants should take into account the changing the nature of cover letters.

Cover letters are much trickier than they used to be. For instance, some job sites don't have options for cover letters to be sent, so most people just don't include one. Other times, resumes are being sent to general e-mail inboxes and again, many job seekers don't feel it to be necessary to send along a cover letter. In the end, you should always, always, always, find some space to put your resume into context and to set it up.

That is the role of the cover letter. By amplifying on information that can be found in the resume, it can be a key means for focusing on your individual qualifications, as well as your interest in a given employer.

COVER LETTER FORMATS

Cover letters share many characteristics of other types of correspondence. Like other letters and memos, they serve as essential communication tools. You might gripe about too much correspondence. You might even laugh at some if it displays bureaucratic or shoddy thinking (the kind that National Public Radio comedian Michael Feldman points out in his humorous book, *Thanks for the Memos*). If you're like most people, much of the correspondence you receive is probably filed promptly in "file 13." But you can't always be on the receiving end. Whenever you're interested in applying for a job, a routine part of your application will be a cover letter designed to accompany your resume or application form.

Before you get involved in the process of writing cover letters, a brief review might be in order. First, consider the basic format of a business letter.

Standard practices for business letters vary slightly depending on what authority is consulted, but expectations for letters generally include the following:

1. **Single-spacing.** Cover letters should always use single-spacing. Double-spacing might be used to set paragraphs apart, and extra spacing normally sets off elements such as the signature. Otherwise, double-spacing in a letter should be avoided.

2. **A recognized format.** Some letter writers prefer a format in which each paragraph is indented five spaces, and the date, closing, and signature are centered. Others use a block style, where paragraphs are not indented and all sections of a letter are flush left (that is, aligned with the left-hand margin). Either format is acceptable. But it is advisable to use one of them rather than developing your own format, which might not be consistent with normal business practices.

3. **Adequate margins.** At least one-inch margins are necessary to maintain an attractive appearance. For extremely brief letters, wider margins might be acceptable to achieve a balance between blank space and text.

BASIC ELEMENTS OF COVER LETTERS

If you have ever been enrolled in a typing or word-processing class, you've probably already covered most of what follows in this section. But this list is offered as a brief refresher, with the added perspective of new options made possible by advancing technology as well as changing social standards. Cover letters, like most other formal letters, include most or all of the following elements:

1. **Letterhead or return address.** In some cases, this will consist of preprinted letterhead stationery. For students or self-employed professionals, it might entail a computer-generated simulation of a traditional letterhead, printed individually with each letter. Or if plain typing paper is used, a return address can simply be typed above the date. Whichever method you choose, a reader should have no difficulty determining where to reach you with a response. This might include phone and e-mail addresses as well as the mailing address, if traditional mail is to be used.

2. **Date.** The day, month, and year should always be listed.

3. **Inside address.** This element hasn't much changed since you were in diapers (other than adjustments in zip codes), but it is as necessary as ever. The main objective here is accuracy. In particular, make sure that names are spelled correctly, even if that means double-checking names against spelling in other documents. Also, try to keep the inside address to no more than four lines, even if the source from which you take it uses a longer version. This will save space in your letter and will also fit better when used to generate envelopes or mailing labels. If necessary, combine information from two lines into one to achieve a shorter address.

4. **Subject line.** An optional element is an attention line or subject line. Some letter writers use these devices to grab the reader's attention. They are most useful in letters directed to large organizations or especially busy people who receive large volumes of mail. In cover letters, the most likely use of an attention line would be to direct a letter to a specific position when you don't know the name of the person you're contacting, or to refer to a specific job opening, as in the following examples:

    Attention: Personnel Director
    RE: Computer Support Technician Position

5. **Salutation.** Writing a salutation seems simple, but advances in gender equity have made this trickier than it once was. "Dear Mr. Gray" seems a foolproof salutation, but what if Gray is a woman? Do you use Mrs., Miss,

or Ms.? Or what if the recipient is named Pat Gray, and you're unsure about gender? (In an issue unrelated to gender, you must also determine whether it is appropriate to use a recipient's given name or surname.)

To avoid offending the reader, follow these simple tips when writing salutations.

- Use a recipient's given (first) name only if you are personally acquainted. It's better to use the more formal Ms. Brown or Mr. Wang than to invoke an artificial level of familiarity.

- For females, use *Ms.* unless you know that the person you are addressing prefers *Miss* or *Mrs.*, or unless *Dr.* or another title is appropriate.

- If you are unsure about gender, try to find out whether the addressee is a male or female (a simple phone call to a secretary, switchboard operator, or company personnel office can often do the trick). If this is not possible, consider using both the given name and the surname in the salutation, as in *Dear Terry Claussen*. An increasingly common practice is simply to omit the salutation. This is one way to avoid gender questions entirely.

- Try to stay on top of academic credentials or other factors related to titles. Don't overlook the use of *Dr.* for people with Ph.D.s; advanced degrees are common among managers in the academic and scientific communities.

- If you do not know the name of the recipient, be creative. Avoid *Dear Sir* (the reader might be a woman) as well as *Dear Sir or Madam* (an outdated phrase). *To Whom It May Concern* is acceptable, if a bit stiff. Instead, try something like *Dear Personnel Director* or *Dear Human Resources Manager*.

6. **Body.** The body of a cover letter can vary from one to several paragraphs in length, but most cover letters are no more than one page long. Normally such a letter will include both an introductory and a concluding statement, as well as the meat of the letter where the main point is made. The body is where your writing prowess counts most.

7. **Complimentary close.** No, this is not some kind of freebie. It's just another convention of business correspondence, where you wind up your letter on a courteous note. Phrases such as *Sincerely yours* and just *Sincerely* are the norm. *Very truly yours* and *Cordially* may also be used.

   Two points are worth noting here. First, don't get cute with the complimentary close. Phrases such as *Breathlessly awaiting your reply* are out of place. Also, be sure to use lowercase letters for all but the first letter of the initial word in the phrase.

8. **Name and signature.** Your typed name should accompany your signature. Do not omit the typed name, since penmanship can be misinterpreted. Also, use this portion of the letter to emphasize credentials if you feel it's appropriate; designations such as P.E. or Ph.D. can be listed after the typed name. (Note: Avoid overusing such designations. Even if you have worked hard to earn them, it is unbecoming to note them unless there is a specific reason to do so, such as a desire to emphasize your credentials to a possible employer in addition to including such information in your resume.)

   Also, don't overlook the importance of the signature. If you're trying to convey a friendly or informal tone, consider signing only your first name and omitting the last name. Both names appear anyway in the typed line below your signature; leaving out the last name in your signature provides a subtle measure of informality, when appropriate.

Of course in electronic versions, a signature might not apply. Even though software might allow you to simulate a signature, that might be off-putting to some recipients.. The best option is simply to leave a blank space where the signature would go.

9. **Notations.** Special notations, such as the initials of a typist or indications of who will receive copies, are also holdovers from traditional letters. For example, CC is an abbreviation of *carbon copy*. Even though carbon paper is an outdated technology, the notation is still frequently used for any type of copy.

Common notations used in business letters include the following (it's unlikely that you will use most of them in a typical cover letter, but you might):

CC or cc: carbon copy
c: copy
BCC or bcc: blind copy
pc: private copy—same as blind copy
ENCL or encl: enclosure

CONTENT BASICS

While cover letters follow the same basic format as other business letters, they also tend to have their own formula when it comes to content. Of course, the basic content might vary depending on your own stylistic preferences. The main consideration will be how much information you want to convey in the letter as opposed to the resume or other material it accompanies. In general, any letter will include most or all of these elements:

■ An opening statement of your interest in being considered for a job
■ A reference to your resume or other enclosures
■ A comment or two about your qualifications or suitability for the job
■ A closing statement emphasizing your availability for an interview or further discussion
■ Enclosures or attachments

An opening paragraph should explain why the letter is being written. Keep in mind that most businesspeople receive more mail than they would like. They tend to read quickly, but not necessarily thoroughly. Also, on the same day that your letter and resume arrive, a busy manager might receive plenty of mail from other sources. To make certain your letter is both read and comprehended, make certain that the opening paragraph reveals exactly why you have taken the time to write; in other words, convey that you are interested in a specific job and that your resume is being provided.

A middle section (one or more paragraphs) can then convey the main message of the letter. This usually consists of a few comments about your qualifications. Typically, this section highlights, clarifies, or enhances information presented in a resume (more details on this later).

A closing sentence or paragraph should clarify the writer's expectations and sum up the main purpose of the letter. Here, you clearly state what is being asked of the reader in terms of understanding or follow-up. For a letter expressing interest in a job, this is usually a reminder of your availability and a note of thanks for being considered.

Qualities of a Slam Dunk Cover Letter

- Is neat and readable
- Conforms to standard business practices
- Sets up your enclosure
- Presents your case for employment without duplicating material in your resume
- Is precise and concise
- Uses strong, clear language
- Calls attention to special points of interest
- Makes you look highly competent

MAINTAINING THE RIGHT APPEARANCE

Saying the right words in a letter is vital. A more mundane consideration, but also an important one, is the overall appearance of cover letters. Before finalizing any letter, be sure to consider these elements.

For traditional letters that are to be mailed rather than submitted electronically, factors such as the type of paper to use might seem insignificant. But in a competitive job search, everything counts, at least potentially. Here are some factors to consider.

1. **Size.** Always use standard, 8-1/2-by-11-inch sheets of paper. Smaller sizes might be appropriate for some types of letters (for example, a thank-you note on personalized, 6-by-9-inch stationery can be effective). But cover letters should be the same size as the resumes they are designed to accompany. Standard-sized paper is easier to file, less likely to be misplaced, and less apt to draw unfavorable reactions from conservative readers. Also, with smaller paper, the eye might be drawn away from the cover letter to the material it accompanies. This runs contrary to the desired order; you want the letter to be read first, then the resume.

    There is no reason to use paper larger than 8 by 11 inches.

2. **Color.** Plain white paper is best. Some people like to use light shades of gray or tan, especially if they have gone to the trouble of obtaining professionally printed stationery. This is generally acceptable, although white is more widely preferred in the business community.

    Avoid pastel colors, bright hues, or other attention-getters. A cover letter is no place to make a fashion statement. Rather, in appearance and format each letter should be simple and businesslike. Remember that because you rarely know the individual preferences of employers, it's important to stay on the conservative side to avoid offending people with traditional preferences for business correspondence. If you want to assert your individuality, focus on content and develop a Type B letter (discussed in Chapter 3).

    Also, keep in mind that colors other than white sometimes do not photocopy well; this can be a problem if your letter is copied to be shared with several staff members.

3. **Weight.** Expensive paper can be attractive, but it is not necessary. On the other hand, avoid light, flimsy paper that looks cheap. At a minimum, choose 20-pound paper (the kind suitable for copiers).

4. **Personalized letterhead.** Do you need personalized stationery with your name and address professionally printed? Some writers suggest this strategy as a way of looking professional. But it isn't really necessary. Ordinary typing paper will be fine as long as the material it contains meets the standards discussed earlier.

   If you do opt for personal stationery, go for simplicity. Use a simple typeface, and stay away from logos or other graphic designs. Be sure to choose stationery that matches the paper you use for your resume.

Selecting Envelopes

A plain business envelope is your best choice, unless you have purchased envelopes designed to match personalized stationery. You need not buy expensive envelopes to make a good impression on a potential employer. As long as the address is neatly typed and the envelope is not of an unusual size or design, it should be acceptable.

If you are enclosing a resume that is several pages long, or if other documents (such as an application form) are enclosed, consider keeping your material flat instead of folding it before mailing. This will require using a 9-by-12-inch envelope. Here, you will need to prepare an address label and attach it to the envelope. Do not send handwritten envelopes.

SPECIAL TIPS FOR ELECTRONIC SUBMISSIONS

If you submit a cover letter electronically, take time to consider how you can best adapt it to that medium. Lena Bottos, a compensation consultant for Salary.com, Inc., offers these tips:

- Don't forget that your cover letter will most likely be printed out. While it might look good on your computer screen, the printed version of it might be a disaster. Be sure that both the electronic and printed formats are pleasing to the eye. Some tricks are:
  - ❑ After you type your e-mail, try making the e-mail window wider and narrower by dragging the right hand side of the window. Look for what happens at the ends of the lines of text. Often you'll see one or two words on every other line.
  - ❑ E-mail the message to yourself first at one or two different accounts to see how a recipient might see it.
  - ❑ Most business e-mail systems support HTML formatted e-mails or RTF (rich text format) e-mails. You can use these formats to improve the presentation of your e-mail beyond the standard courier text e-mails. With these format options, you can use bold, italics, and bullets, all of which can make your e-mail stand out and allow you to properly highlight the most important aspects of your cover letter. Keep your formatting simple, though. Avoid using special characters because not all programs will interpret them properly, and some corporate e-mail programs might even convert your e-mail to plain text format.

❑ Make your e-mail brief and attach a cover letter in MS Word or a PDF.

■ Cover letters are used to catch the eye of a potential employer. Make sure that the most important points in your cover letter sit "above the fold," that is everything you want someone to notice should appear on the first screen of the letter. It shouldn't be necessary to scroll to get to the most valuable information.

■ Set up an e-mail address that is a combination of your first and last name. This is free to do and is more professional than a funny (or embarrassing) nickname. Also, check to see how your name appears in others' e-mail inboxes. With public e-mail services, you can control how your name appears so that the recipient will see your first name and last name rather than a nickname or just your e-mail address. (In your e-mail account, change your personalization options for "alias" or "from name.")

■ Don't overlook the importance of an informative subject. Include your name and position you want to interview for. Make sure your subject line looks personal and professional, not like spam. Look to see if the posting states what the subject line should be because that will often be used on the receiving end to filter the responses. If you have the wrong subject, you might not get into the queue.

3
Two Basic Styles of Cover Letters

Effective cover letters come in two basic varieties. You can use either or both, depending on your own personality and the types of employers you will be approaching.

TYPE A

The Always Appropriate letter. If you want to play it safe, this is the best type of cover letter to use when applying for a job. Just as you dress in your best (and perhaps most conservative) clothes when going on a job interview, you employ the Type A letter when trying to convey a solid, no-nonsense image.

Type A letters represent the mainstream of business communication. They are polite and formal. Typically, they show deference to the employer. The general tone of a Type A letter is respectful and cooperative.

TYPE B

The Bold and Brassy letter. What if a man showed up for a job interview wearing a bright green blazer, a yellow tie, and tan slacks? Or if a woman went to her interview in a flashy pantsuit and a floppy hat?

Let's face it, this would be the kiss of death for some job situations. Even though you might argue that clothes aren't really relevant to job performance, many employers would not look favorably on anything other than conservative business attire.

Some employers, on the other hand, would feel just the opposite. Your clothes might happen to mesh with their personal tastes. Or such clothes might be a good match for the particular culture of a given organization. Perhaps they simply seem right for your personality, and the employer will find it refreshing that you are not exactly like everyone else.

The situation is similar with Type B cover letters. They are somewhat different from traditional Type A letters in style and approach. For example, when writing a Type B letter, you might do any or all of the following:

- Start out with a clever opening designed to catch the reader's attention.
- Use an anecdote or quotation to make a point about your interest in (or suitability for) a given position.
- Vary the format or layout by including lists, one-sentence paragraphs, or other variations from the traditional letter format.
- Use informal language.
- Express a strong opinion.
- Ask a question.

Examples of these methods can be found in the sample cover letters presented later in this book. As you develop your own versions, keep in mind that the more you deviate from the traditional Type A letter format, the more risk you take. It's possible that readers could find you flippant instead of clever, flaky instead of creative, or suspiciously nonconformist instead of innovative. On the other hand, a Type B cover letter that hits its mark might be just the catalyst you need to bring success. If you're willing to assume a little risk, the Type B style can be effective.

Before trying this kind of cover letter, ask yourself these questions.

- Do I have a better chance at revealing my own personality than I would with a traditional Type A letter?
- Will a Bold and Brassy letter make my application stand out in comparison to others?
- How strong is the possibility that an employer will be turned off by my nontraditional approach to letter writing? Am I willing to take this risk?

TWO STYLES OF COVER LETTERS

	Type A: Always Appropriate	Type B: Bold and Brassy
Description:	Formal. Conservative.	Informal. Flashy.
Strengths:	Always appropriate for any audience.	Stands out from letters submitted by other applicants.

	Appeals to employers with traditional business values.	Appeals to those who enjoy creative approaches.
	Makes you appear well organized and businesslike.	Makes you appear original and innovative.
	Can easily be adapted for submission to multiple employers.	Features individualized ties to specific jobs.
Weaknesses:	Might be boring for all readers/audiences.	Might not be appropriate.
	Might not stand out from letters submitted by other applicants.	Might bring a negative reaction.

EXAMPLES OF SLAM DUNK COVER LETTERS

Following are samples of both Type A and Type B slam dunk cover letters. The first of each pair is a Type A (Always Appropriate) example. The second is Type B (Bold and Brassy).

Look these over and make your own assessment of which works best. Then make your own stylistic choices. In the process, feel free to borrow from any phrasing or organizational features you feel might work well in your own cover letters.

Also, feel free to adapt these for use in e-mail messages or Internet job sites. While the format might vary, the same concepts apply.

More examples of slam dunk cover letters appear later in this book.

KRISTEN ADAMS
188 Cooper Lane Extension
High Point, NC 27261
(910) 555-5934
kadams@xxx.com

March 12, 20__

Dr. Paul Lawson, President
Lawson Environmental Enterprises
618 Reading Road
Marietta, Maine 04401

Dear Dr. Lawson:

The enclosed resume is submitted in application for the position of Research Coordinator as advertised in the *News Journal*.

I believe my solid background in research provides a good match for the duties required for this position. While employed with two progressive biotechnology companies, I specialized in performing duties quite similar to those listed in your job description.

In addition to my professional background, I have long been interested in the environment and have served in several leadership capacities with state and national organizations related to environmental protection. I would enjoy being associated with a firm such as your own, which has an obvious commitment to environmental preservation.

If you would like to schedule an interview or otherwise discuss my interest in this position, please call me at the number listed above. I will be available at your convenience.

Thank you for your consideration.

Sincerely,

Kristen Adams, Ph.D.

KRISTEN ADAMS

188 Cooper Lane Extension
High Point, NC 27261
(910) 555-5934
kadams@xxx.com

March 12, 20___

Dr. Paul Lawson, President
Lawson Environmental Enterprises
517 Reading Road
Marietta, Maine 04401

Dear Dr. Lawson:

Nothing is more important to a technology-based company than creative, disciplined, thorough research. You know it, and I know it. What's more, I can help your company reach new heights in this area. That's why I'm submitting the enclosed resume in application for the position of Research Coordinator, as advertised in the *News Journal*.

I believe my solid background in research provides a good match for the duties required of this position. While employed with two progressive biotechnology companies, I specialized in performing duties quite similar to those listed in your job announcement.

In addition to my professional background, I have long been interested in the environment and have served in several leadership capacities with state and national organizations related to environmental protection. I'd really enjoy being associated with a firm such as your own with an obvious commitment to environmental preservation.

If you'd like to schedule an interview or otherwise discuss my interest in this position, please call me at the number listed above. I'm available at your convenience.

Thank you for your consideration.

Sincerely,

Kristen Adams, Ph.D.

JOSE ALVAREZ

788 Palm Avenue / Canton, OH 44706
(330) 555-2533

June 2, 20__

Janet R. Foley, Human Resources Manager
Western Trucking, Inc.
35 East Howard
Cincinnati, OH 45237-3806

Dear Ms. Foley:

I understand that your company operates a substantial truck repair operation as part of a general fleet maintenance program. I'm an experiencμed specialist in diesel engine repair as well as other aspects of truck maintenance, and as such would like to offer my services should a position become available.

Enclosed is a copy of my resume. You will see that I have nearly six years of experience in performing a variety of tasks related to repairing and maintaining large trucks. Most of this work was with IntraState Truck Services, where I performed with distinction and received excellent evaluations from my superiors.

If a position becomes open with your company, please consider me. I will be glad to come for an interview if invited, or to provide additional information by mail or telephone.

Thank you for your consideration. I look forward to talking with you.

Very truly yours,

Jose Alvarez

✥ JOSE ALVAREZ ✥
788 Palm Avenue
Canton, OH 44706
(330) 555-2533

June 2, 20__

Janet R. Foley, Human Resources Manager
Western Trucking, Inc.
35 East Howard
Cincinnati, OH 45237-3806

Dear Ms. Foley:

If it's broken, I can fix it.

Well, maybe that's not true for a nuclear reactor. But when you're talking trucks, I really can back up this statement.

As an experienced specialist in diesel engine repair as well as other aspects of truck maintenance, I'd like to offer my services should a position become available.

Enclosed is a copy of my resume. You will see that I have nearly six years of experience in performing a variety of tasks related to repairing and maintaining large trucks. Most of this work was with IntraState Truck Services, where I performed with distinction and received excellent evaluations from my superiors. During this time, I've dealt with just about every imaginable repair situation.

If a position opens within your company, please consider me. I'll be glad to come for an interview if invited, or to provide additional information by mail or telephone.

Thank you for your consideration. I look forward to talking with you.

Very truly yours,

Jose Alvarez

LISA TAYLOR
808 Clarke Avenue
Toronto ON M2M 1H9 Canada
(416) 555-5304
taylors3@xxx.com

July 23, 20___

Anne Garhardt
Personnel and Training Manager
The Darnell Group
4802 Patricia Avenue
Toronto ON M2M 1H8 Canada

Dear Ms. Gerhardt:

Thank you for talking with me today. I enjoyed our telephone conversation.

As you requested, I am enclosing a copy of my resume. This will provide you with specific details regarding my background and qualifications.

You will note that I have a great deal of experience in telemarketing and related work, including conducting telephone surveys for the McGill University and the North American Demographic Association. This background has prepared me to conduct a variety of telephone-based marketing efforts, and I have proven to be a reliable, conscientious, and effective communicator.

I would appreciate the opportunity to meet with you in person to discuss your company's needs for qualified personnel, as well as my capabilities for fulfilling those needs. I will appreciate being considered for any openings that your firm might have. Again, thank you for taking the time to talk with me. I look forward to hearing from you.

Sincerely,

Lisa Taylor

LISA TAYLOR

808 Clarke Avenue
Toronto ON M2M 1H9 Canada
(416) 555-5304
taylors3@xxx.com

July 23, 20__

Anne Garhardt
Personnel and Training Manager
The Darnell Group
4802 Patricia Avenue
Toronto ON M2M 1H8 Canada

Dear Ms. Gerhardt:

Thank you for talking with me today. I enjoyed our conversation.

As you requested, I am enclosing a copy of my resume. This will provide you with specific details regarding my background and qualifications.

Let me point out three good reasons to consider me as a possible employee:

1. *Extensive experience in telemarketing and related work (see details in resume of my work for the McGill University and the North American Demographic Association)*

2. *Excellent communication skills (in looking back on our phone conversation, I hope you will agree I'm articulate and well-spoken)*

3. *Reliability and a strong work ethic (see evaluation information)*

I'd greatly appreciate the chance to meet with you to discuss your company's needs for qualified workers, as well as my capabilities for fulfilling those needs.

Thanks for considering me for any openings that your firm might have. I look forward to hearing from you.

Sincerely,

Lisa Taylor

PAMELA DROSICK

707 Rose Street / Cleveland, OH 44145
(216) 555-8831

October 14, 20__

Ms. Carla Huber
Vice President
Plunkett and Associates
4102 Webster Avenue
Quincy, IL 62301

Dear Ms. Huber:

I am writing to apply for one of the sales openings advertised recently by your company. Enclosed is a resume outlining my background and experience.

I am a self-starter with highly developed skills in setting goals and meeting them. As my resume shows, my background includes several years of successful sales experience. I have been successful in a variety of settings, and can demonstrate excellent planning and communication skills.

I would be interested in any sales position requiring teamwork and a strong work ethic. Those in your eastern district would be of the greatest interest to me, but I would be available at any location.

If you would like to discuss your needs and how I might meet them, please let me know. I will be glad to provide additional details or meet with you for a personal interview.

Thank you for your consideration. I look forward to talking with you.

Sincerely,

Pamela Drosick

❧ PAMELA DROSICK ❧
707 Rose Street
Cleveland, OH 44145
(216) 555-8831

October 14, 20__

Ms. Carla Huber
Vice President
Plunkett and Associates
4102 Webster Avenue
Quincy, IL 62301

Dear Ms. Huber:

You have a job opening. I have a good job but am ready for something more challenging. Can we talk?

Specifically, I'd like to apply for one of the sales openings advertised recently by your company. Enclosed is a resume outlining my background and experience.

I am a self-starter with highly developed skills in setting goals and meeting them. As my resume shows, my background includes several years of successful sales experience. I have been successful in a variety of settings, and can demonstrate excellent planning and communication skills.

I'd be interested in any sales position requiring teamwork and a strong work ethic. Those in your eastern district would be of the greatest interest to me, but I would be available at any location.

If you want to discuss your needs and how I might meet them, please let me know. I'll be glad to provide more details or meet with you for a personal interview.

Thanks for your consideration. I look forward to talking with you.

Sincerely,

Pamela Drosick

DEVON EAST
P.O. Box 1148
Seattle, WA 98101
206) 555-8416
devoneast@xxx.net

November 29, 20__

Ms. Linda Burns, Vice President
Winslow and Associates
84 W. 19th Avenue
Vancouver, BC V5Y 1Z4 Canada

Dear Ms. Burns:

I am writing to apply for the position of fiscal technician, as advertised in Friday's edition of the *Seattle Record.* Enclosed are a resume and the names of three references as requested in the job announcement.

As you will see from the information provided, I have significant previous experience in maintaining financial records. I was employed for three years as a bookkeeper and accounting assistant, a position I left to pursue my bachelor's degree in business administration. Now that my studies have been completed, I am eager to return to full-time employment.

My resume elaborates on these details and other aspects of my qualifications. After reviewing this information, I believe you will agree that my background provides a strong match for the advertised position.

If you need more information or would like me to come for an interview, I am available at your convenience.

Thank you kindly for considering my application. I will look forward to hearing from you.

Yours truly,

Devon East

Devon East

P.O. Box 1148
Seattle, WA 98101
206) 555-8416
devoneast@xxx.net

November 29, 20__

Ms. Linda Burns, Vice President
Winslow and Associates
84 W. 19th Avenue
Vancouver, BC V5Y 1Z4 Canada

Dear Ms. Burns:

College was great, but now I'm ready to return to the real world! So please consider me for the position of fiscal technician as advertised in Friday's edition of the *Seattle Record*. Enclosed are a resume and the names of three references as requested.

As you will see from the information provided, I have significant previous experience in maintaining financial records. I was employed for three years as a bookkeeper and accounting assistant, a position I left to pursue my bachelor's degree in business administration. Now that my studies have been completed, I am eager to return to full-time employment.

My resume elaborates on these details and other aspects of my qualifications. After reviewing this information, I believe you will agree that my background provides a strong match for the advertised position.

If you need more information or would like me to come for an interview, I'm available at your convenience.

Thank you kindly for considering my application. I look forward to hearing from you.

Yours truly,

Devon East

Kim O'Hara
946 Damon Road
Manchester, NH 03105
Kim22@xxx.com

February 11, 20__

Mr. Alvin Patterson, General Manager
East Coast Manufacturing
490 W. Martin Pike
Cherry Hill, NJ 08003

Dear Mr. Patterson:

Please accept the enclosed resume in application for the position of training director at your organization. This is in response to the job vacancy notice published this week in the *New York Times*.

As you will gather from my resume, I have a great deal of experience in corporate training. In fact, I believe that my professional background provides the ideal qualifications you are seeking.

If you would like more information, please contact me. I am available for an interview at your convenience. My telephone number is (603) 555-9737, and I can be reached there at any time through my voice mail service or at the e-mail address noted above.

Thank you for your consideration. I look forward to your response.

Sincerely,

Kim O'Hara

⚜ Kim O'Hara ⚜
946 Damon Road
Manchester, NH 03105
Kim22@xxx.com

February 11, 20__

Mr. Alvin Patterson, General Manager
East Coast Manufacturing
490 W. Martin Pike
Cherry Hill, NJ 08003

Dear Mr. Patterson:

I have noted with interest your company's slogan that "people are our greatest asset." Well, I'm definitely a "people person," and I get a kick out of working closely with employees to help them acquire new job skills. That's why I'm responding to the *New York Times* ad for a new training director at your organization.

As you'll gather from my resume, I have a great deal of experience in corporate training. In fact, I believe that my professional background provides the ideal qualifications you are seeking.

If you would like more information, please contact me. I am available for an interview at your convenience. My telephone number is (603) 555-9737, and I can be reached there at any time through my voice mail service, or at the e-mail address noted above.

Thank you for your consideration. I look forward to your response.

Sincerely,

Kim O'Hara

PAUL DAWSON
P.O. Box 914
Statesville, NC 28687-0914
(704) 555-7102

February 3, 20__

Ms. Angela Covey
Human Resources Manager
The Bly Corporation
1148 Dyer Boulevard
West Palm Beach, FL 33407

Dear Ms. Covey:

Enclosed is my resume for your consideration. I am interested in obtaining employment in your operations in North Carolina, South Carolina, or Virginia. I would like the opportunity to apply for any positions that may become open in the near future.

I am in the process of completing a bachelor's degree in business administration at North Carolina State University. Although I am currently enrolled as a full-time student, I am available for employment immediately following completion of the current semester. I am also willing to relocate.

I believe that my training and strong work ethic will allow me to make a significant contribution to your company. Please let me know if you would like more information about my qualifications.

I hope you will consider me for any appropriate position, and I look forward to hearing from you. Thank you for your consideration.

Sincerely yours,

Paul Dawson

PAUL DAWSON

P.O. Box 914
Statesville, NC 28687-0914
(704) 555-7102

February 3, 20___

Ms. Angela Covey
Human Resources Manager
The Bly Corporation
1148 Dyer Boulevard
West Palm Beach, FL 33407

Dear Ms. Covey:

As a prospective college graduate, I realize that you probably have job applicants with many more years of experience than I can offer. But please take a few minutes to look at my resume (copy enclosed). You'll see that I can bring several distinct skills to your organization.

I am in the process of completing a bachelor's degree in business administration at North Carolina State University. Although I am currently enrolled as a full-time student, I am available for employment immediately following completion of the current semester. I am also willing to relocate. Of special interest would be any suitable openings in your operations in North Carolina, South Carolina, or Virginia. I would be interested in applying for any such positions that may become open in the near future.

I believe that my training and strong work ethic will allow me to make a significant contribution to your company. Please let me know if you would like more information about my qualifications.

I hope you will consider me for any appropriate position, and I look forward to hearing from you. Thank you for your consideration.

Sincerely yours,

Paul Dawson

Two Basic Styles of Cover Letters

Chris Dixon

62 Lakeside Apartments / Gurnee, IL 60031
(847) 555-8216 / (847) 555-9944 (fax)

April 12, 20__

Michael Chinn, Vice President
KBT Financial Services
3245 N. Kolin Avenue
Chicago, IL 60632

Dear Mr. Chinn:

Thank you for taking the time to talk with me yesterday about employment possibilities with your firm. Your enthusiasm about KBT must be contagious, for I am highly interested in following up on our conversation.

Enclosed for your review is a copy of my resume. You will see, as we discussed, that I have had four years of experience as a successful full-service insurance agent, as well as appropriate academic preparation.

I am a hard worker who enjoys dealing with the public. I have excellent communication skills as well as strong organizational capabilities.

Please review my background and call me at the number listed above if you would like to talk further. I would be available for an interview at any time.

Thank you for your consideration.

Sincerely,

Chris Dixon

❧ Chris Dixon ❧

62 Lakeside Apartments
Gurnee, IL 60031
(847) 555-8216
(847) 555-9944 (fax)

April 12, 20__

Michael Chinn, Vice President
KBT Financial Services
3245 N. Kolin Avenue
Chicago, IL 60632

Dear Mr. Chinn:

Thank you for taking the time to talk with me yesterday about employment possibilities with your firm. Your enthusiasm about KBT must be contagious, for I am highly interested in following up on our conversation.

Enclosed for your review is a copy of my resume. You will see, as we discussed, that:

- I have had four years of successful experience as a full-service insurance agent.

- My academic preparation is right in line with the expectations of your company.

- My current employer has cited me as a hard worker with excellent communication skills and strong organizational capabilities.

Please review my background and call me at the number listed above if you would like to talk further. I would be available for an interview at any time.

Thank you for your consideration.

Sincerely,

Chris Dixon

JAMES YAMAGUCHI
1305 Fraley Street, Apartment 18
Charlotte, NC 28217
(704) 555-3480
yamaman@xxx.com

April 26, 20__

Althea Smythe
Executive Assistant to the President
Appleton Pharmacies
1414 The Exchange
Atlanta, GA 30339

Dear Ms. Smythe:

I am writing to express my interest in obtaining a position with your company. I am familiar with your organization as a customer, and I have always been impressed with your operations.

A copy of my resume is enclosed. As you will see, I am an experienced pharmacy technician with the requisite training and background. I am skilled in providing an array of support services for pharmacy operations.

If you have any openings now or in the near future, I would appreciate being considered. I would be glad to provide additional application materials upon request.

Thank you for considering my application. I hope to hear from you soon.

Yours sincerely,

James Yamaguchi

Enclosure: Resume

JAMES YAMAGUCHI

1305 Fraley Street, Apartment 18
Charlotte, NC 28217
(704) 555-3480
yamaman@xxx.com

April 26, 20__

Althea Smythe
Executive Assistant to the President
Appleton Pharmacies
1414 The Exchange
Atlanta, GA 30339

Dear Ms. Smythe:

I believe it was Milton Berle who said, "If opportunity doesn't knock, build a door." That is why I'm writing to you today. Although your company is not currently advertising for new employees, I'd like to introduce myself in the event that openings do occur. I am familiar with your organization as a customer, and I have always been impressed with your operations.

A copy of my resume is enclosed. As you will see, I'm an experienced pharmacy technician with the requisite training and background. I am skilled in providing an array of support services for pharmacy operations.

If you have any openings now or in the near future, I would appreciate being considered. I'd be glad to provide additional application materials upon request.

Thanks for considering my application. I hope to hear from you at your convenience.

Yours sincerely,

James Yamaguchi

Enclosure: Resume

DIANE GRAVES

P.O. Box 6055
Des Plaines, IL 60017
(847) 555-2787

September 15, 20__

Mr. Jason Ziegler, President
Ziegler-Johnson Enterprises
4522 Teamster Street
Des Plaines, IL 60017

Dear Mr. Ziegler:

As you may recall, I spoke with you last year regarding possible employment with your firm following completion of my studies at the University of Illinois. Now that my degree is in hand, I would like to express interest in employment at this time.

Enclosed is a copy of my resume for your perusal. As you will note, in addition to my bachelor's degree in business administration, I have had considerable management experience through internships and part-time employment. It is my hope to build upon this background by working in a leading firm such as your own.

I would appreciate the opportunity to talk with you in person to discuss your firm's needs for aggressive, hardworking employees. Please let me know if I can provide additional information.

I look forward to hearing from you.

Sincerely yours,

Diane Graves

❧ *Diane Graves* ❧
P.O. Box 6055
Des Plaines, IL 60017
(847) 555-2787

April 26, 20__

Mr. Jason Ziegler, President
Ziegler-Johnson Enterprises
4522 Teamster Street
Des Plaines, IL 60017

Dear Mr. Ziegler:

Can you remember every phone conversation you had last year? I can't. But since it was so important to my future, there is one I recall quite distinctly.

I spoke with you last year regarding possible employment with your firm following completion of my studies at the University of Illinois. You were nice enough to encourage me to contact you when my degree was in hand. So now that I have graduated, I'd like to express interest in employment at this time.

Enclosed is a copy of my resume for your perusal. As you will note, in addition to my bachelor's degree in business administration, I have had considerable management experience through internships and part-time employment. It is my hope to build upon this background by working in a leading firm such as your own.

I'd appreciate the opportunity to talk with you in person to discuss your firm's needs for aggressive, hardworking employees. Please let me know if I can provide additional information.

I look forward to hearing from you.

Sincerely yours,

Diane Graves

BRIAN DODSON
1111 Main Street
Woodland Hills, CA 91367
(818) 555-5064
dodson22@xxx.net

January 17, 20___

Ms. Betty Hamilton, Creative Director
Aldrich Advertising
743 Enterprise Road
Pomona, CA 91768

Dear Ms. Hamilton:

Please accept this letter and the enclosed resume in application for the position of copywriter announced this week.

I believe that my extensive background in writing advertising copy provides a good match for the requirements described in your job announcement. I am experienced in developing a wide range of material, including print ads, radio and television commercials, annual reports, and various other publications. I'm confident I could help meet your demand for well-written material.

Please review my resume and let me know if you feel my background fits with the needs of your company. I would appreciate the chance to talk with you about this position at your convenience.

Yours truly,

Brian Dodson

BRIAN DODSON

1111 Main Street
Woodland Hills, CA 91367
(818) 555-5064
dodson22@xxx.net

January 17, 20__

Ms. Betty Hamilton, Creative Director
Aldrich Advertising
743 Enterprise Road
Pomona, CA 91768

Dear Ms. Hamilton:

Do you find it difficult to supervise creative people? If so, please give careful consideration to my application. I am a highly creative copywriter (with the clips and awards to prove it), but I'm also a cooperative, personable team player who has been cited as an exemplary employee by two supervisors.

With that brief introduction, please accept this letter and the enclosed resume in application for the position of copywriter announced this week.

I believe that my extensive background in writing advertising and public relations copy provides a good match for the requirements described in your job announcement. I'm experienced in developing a wide range of material including print ads, radio and television commercials, annual reports, and various other publications. I'll be glad to provide clips, copies of my performance evaluations, or any other details you might request.

Please review my resume and let me know if you feel my background fits with the needs of your company. I would appreciate the chance to talk with you about this position at your convenience.

Yours truly,

Brian Dodson

BRAD TAYLOR

634 Seventh Avenue Extension
Pittsburgh, PA 15219
Telephone: (412) 555-7122

January 30, 20__

Donna Vicars
Knox Support Services
1642 M Street
Philadelphia, PA 19124-9962

Dear Ms. Vicars:

As one who is eager to advance my career in sales and marketing, I am submitting the enclosed resume for your review. I would appreciate being considered as an addition to your staff.

My background includes both retail sales and experience as a recruiter for a four-year college. In both capacities, I have gained invaluable background in self-motivation, time management, communication skills, and other attributes vital to successful marketing.

I am a diligent worker who enjoys learning new skills and techniques. My positive attitude and emphasis on teamwork would be valuable assets for your organization.

I will be very grateful for the chance to talk with you about your company's needs and how I might meet them. I am available at your convenience.

Thanks very much for your consideration.

Sincerely,

Brad Taylor

❧ BRAD TAYLOR ❧
634 Seventh Avenue Extension
Pittsburgh, PA 15219
Telephone: (412) 555-7122

January 30, 20__

Donna Vicars
Knox Support Services
1642 M Street
Philadelphia, PA 19124-9962

Dear Ms. Vicars:

"Obstacles," said Joseph Cossman, "are things a person sees when he takes his eyes off the goal." Well, I seldom take my eye off the goal, and as a result I don't let obstacles get in my way. That's why I'm a record-setting salesman at my company.

I would now like to build on this success by moving to a large, progressive company such as your own. Thus I'm submitting the enclosed resume for your review. I would appreciate being considered as an addition to your staff.

My background includes both retail sales and experience as a recruiter for a four-year college. In both capacities, I have gained invaluable background in self-motivation, time management, communication skills, and other attributes vital to successful marketing.

I am a diligent worker who enjoys learning new skills and techniques. My positive attitude and emphasis on teamwork would be valuable assets for your organization.

I will be very grateful for the chance to talk with you about your company's needs and how I might meet them. I am available at your convenience.

Thanks very much for your consideration.

Sincerely,

Brad Taylor

JOE C. POWELL
110 Walton Way
Bayshore, NY 11705
(516) 555-4874

July 20, 20__

Kathey Ramesy-Smith
Human Resources Coordinator
LaMotte Technical Services
116 Spur Drive N.
Bayshore, NY 11706

Dear Ms. Ramsey-Smith:

I understand that your firm employs a number of computer repair technicians. I have recently completed an associate degree in computer technology at Bayshore Technical College, where I acquired a variety of maintenance and repair skills. Now that my studies have concluded, I am eager to apply my capabilities in the workplace.

Enclosed is a copy of my resume. As you will see, I have training in a broad range of tasks needed for working with contemporary computers and related equipment. I'm a team player with excellent work habits, outstanding technical capabilities, and a thorough, dedicated approach to work.

I would be most interested in discussing with you any opportunities for employment with your firm. Please contact me if you would like additional information.

Thank you for your consideration.

                                        Sincerely,

                                        Joe C. Powell

JOE C. POWELL

110 Walton Way
Bayshore, NY 11705
(516) 555-4874

July 20, 20__

Kathy Ramsey-Smith, Human Resources Coordinator
LaMotte Technical Services
116 Spur Drive N.
Bayshore, NY 11706

Dear Ms. Ramsey-Smith:

Computers are great. But not when they're on the blink.

Some people curse broken computers. Others throw up their hands and walk away. Not me. I fix them.

Thus my letter and the enclosed resume. I have recently completed an associate degree in computer technology at Bayshore Technical College, where I acquired a variety of maintenance and repair skills. Now that my studies have concluded, I am eager to apply my capabilities in the workplace.

As my resume notes, I have training in a broad range of tasks needed for working with contemporary computers and related equipment. I'm a team player with excellent work habits, outstanding technical capabilities, and a thorough, dedicated approach to work.

I would be most interested in discussing with you any opportunities for employment with your firm. Please contact me if you'd like additional information.

Thanks for your consideration.

Sincerely,

Joe C. Powell

JAMES PATE

132 BROOKVIEW PLACE / CANTON, OH 44706
(330) 555-2533
E-mail: patejs@xxx.net

May 21, 20__

Elaine R. Owens, Vice President
Western Printing and Publishing
35 East Howard
Cincinnati, OH 45237-3806

Dear Ms. Owens:

This is to inquire about possible employment with your company. I am planning to relocate to the Cincinnati area soon, and I would be very interested in joining your staff should a position become available.

My background in the printing field includes three years of experience with Smith Printers here in Canton, where I have performed a wide range of printing services. My experience has included operating various types of printing equipment while utilizing a teamwork approach in providing excellent service.

Enclosed is a copy of my resume for your review. If you would like additional information, I'll be glad to provide it. Please let me know if you would like for me to meet with you in person to discuss your employment needs.

Thank you for considering my resume. I hope to hear from you soon.

Sincerely,

James Pate

Enclosure

❧ JAMES PATE ❧
132 BROOKVIEW PLACE / CANTON, OH 44706
(330) 555-2533 / E-mail: patejs@xxx.net

May 21, 20__

Elaine R. Owens, Vice President
Western Printing and Publishing
35 East Howard
Cincinnati, OH 45237-3806

Dear Ms. Owns:

Canton is a nice town, but it doesn't hold a candle to Cincinnati. At least that's what my wife says, and she has convinced me to relocate to your area. The fact that her employers have just offered her a promotion at their Cincinnati office may also have something to do with it.

At any rate, with this move imminent, I'd like to inquire about possible employment with your company. I would be very interested in joining your staff should a position become available.

My background in the printing field includes three years of experience with Smith Printers here in Canton, where I have performed a wide range of printing services. My experience has included operating various types of printing equipment while utilizing a teamwork approach in providing excellent service.

Enclosed is a copy of my resume for your review. If you would like additional information, I'll be glad to provide it. Please let me know if you would like for me to meet with you in person to discuss your employment needs.

Thank you for considering my resume. I hope to hear from you soon.

Sincerely,

James Pate
Enclosure

ANNE B. CHAN
401 Diller Avenue
New Holland, PA 17557
(717) 555-3465

March 21, 20__

Mr. Lewis Martin, Vice President
NCP Enterprises
108 Oregon Avenue
Wilkes-Barre, PA 18702

Dear Mr. Martin:

Thank you for the information you sent me about your firm. Your company's accomplishments are most impressive.

A copy of my resume is enclosed for your review. As you can see, I have had a highly successful career as an educator. I would now like to apply the leadership and communication skills I've developed over twelve years to the financial services field. I have been preparing for this career change for some time; this year I completed a master's degree in finance with a specialty in investment management.

I believe that my skills and training would be an asset to your company as you position your organization in an increasingly competitive market. My skills should be particularly useful in your efforts to market financial products to those in the educational community.

I am available at the phone number listed above during evening hours. If you need to contact me during the day, I can be reached at 555-2335. Please let me know if you would like to talk further, or if I can provide additional information.

Sincerely yours,

Anne B. Chan

ANNE B. CHAN

401 Diller Avenue
New Holland, PA 17557
(717) 555-3465

March 21, 20__

Mr. Lewis Martin, Vice President
NCP Enterprises
108 Oregon Avenue
Wilkes-Barre, PA 18702

Dear Mr. Martin:

Some people say working in the education field separates you from the real world. I disagree. In fact, I'm convinced that teaching develops skills that can be applied in other fields of endeavor, from planning and organizing complex information to communicating effectively with others.

As an educator who also has a long-standing interest in the financial world, I would be interested in exploring possible employment with your company. A copy of my resume is enclosed for your review.

As you can see, I have had a highly successful career as a teacher. I would now like to apply the leadership and communication skills developed over twelve years of teaching to the financial services field. I have been preparing for this career change for some time; this year I completed a master's degree in finance with a specialty in investment management.

I believe that my experience and training would be an asset to your company as you position your firm in an increasingly competitive market. My skills should be particularly useful in your efforts to market financial products to those in the educational community.

I am available at the phone number listed above during evening hours. If you need to reach me during the day, I can be contacted at 555-2335. Please let me know if you would like to talk further, or if I can provide additional information.

Sincerely yours,

Anne B. Chan

JOSH E. MARTIN

501 Middleview Lane / Rapid City, SD 57701
(605) 555-3361

October 9, 20__

Janet Mercer, Director of Personnel Services
Hastings & Thompson Clinical Associates
303 Transit Street
West Des Moines, IA 50266

Dear Ms. Mercer:

I enjoyed talking with you yesterday about the counseling position that was advertised in *The Daily Mail*. I am definitely interested in being considered for the position.

Enclosed for your review is a copy of my resume. You will note that I have had significant experience in providing a variety of counseling services, with extensive experience in substance abuse counseling. My academic background also provides a good match with your requirements.

If you would like more information, please let me know. I would be happy to expand on my qualifications and interests through a personal interview.

If you would like to discuss this matter, please contact me by mail or telephone. I look forward to hearing from you.

Sincerely,

Josh E. Martin

Enclosure: Resume

❧ JOSH E. MARTIN ❧
501 Middleview Lane
Rapid City, SD 57701
(605) 555-3361

October 9, 20__

Janet Mercer, Director of Personnel Services
Hastings & Thompson Clinical Associates
303 Transit Street
West Des Moines, IA 50266

Dear Ms. Mercer:

Everyone knows that substance abuse is a real problem. But not everyone can help people deal with the complex issues related to drug and alcohol abuse. In fact, many otherwise competent counselors are nonplussed when it comes to helping clients with this issue.

For me, substance abuse counseling is a specialty. That is why I was most interested to see this emphasis for the counseling position that was advertised in *The Daily Mail*. I enjoyed talking with you yesterday about the job and am definitely interested in being considered.

Enclosed for your review is a copy of my resume. You will note that I have had significant experience in substance abuse counseling as well as a variety of other counseling services. My academic background also provides a good match with your needs.

If you would like more information, please let me know. I'll be glad to expand on my qualifications and interests through a personal interview.

If you would like to discuss this matter, please contact me by mail or telephone. I look forward to hearing from you.

Sincerely,

Josh E. Martin
Enclosure: Resume

MARIA S. PEREZ
1411 Ninth Street
Newport Beach, CA 92663
(714) 555-6584 (voice mail)
(714) 555-6686 (fax)

April 16, 20__

Mr. Jeffrey Kleppin, Senior Partner
Darnow, Darnow and Olsen
411 Broadway Plaza
Oakland, CA 94608

Dear Mr. Kleppin:

I am very interested in obtaining employment with a progressive legal firm such as your own through which I might utilize my skills as a trained paralegal. Accordingly, I am submitting this letter in application for the position currently being advertised.

As the enclosed resume indicates, I have just completed an extensive training program in paralegal studies, and have served two internships in attorneys' offices. I am now ready to apply my training and experience through full-time employment in a legal setting.

While you may have applicants with more experience, I can assure you that you will find no one with greater diligence or more enthusiasm. If given the opportunity, I could bring a high level of dedication to the job.

I will appreciate your reviewing my credentials relative to your requirements. If you would like more information, or if you would like to arrange an interview, please contact me. I look forward to hearing from you.

Sincerely,

Maria S. Perez

MARIA S. PEREZ

1411 Ninth Street
Newport Beach, CA 92663
(714) 555-6584 (voice mail)
(714) 555-6686 (fax)

April 16, 20__

Mr. Jeffrey Kleppin, Senior Partner
Darnow, Darnow and Olsen
411 Broadway Plaza
Oakland, CA 94608

Dear Mr. Kleppin:

Before going any further, let me say this: I never tell lawyer jokes (as for golf jokes, that's another matter). To the contrary, I like and respect attorneys. And I have made it a goal to work for a progressive legal firm such as your own. Thus I am submitting this letter in application for the recently advertised paralegal position.

As the enclosed resume indicates, I have just completed an extensive training program in paralegal studies, and have served two internships in attorneys' offices. I am now ready to apply my training and experience through full-time employment in a legal setting.

I realize you may have applicants with more experience. But let me assure you of this: you will find *no one* with greater diligence or more enthusiasm. If given the opportunity, I guarantee that I will bring a high level of dedication to the job.

I will appreciate your reviewing my credentials relative to your requirements. If you'd like more information, or if you want to arrange an interview, please contact me. I look forward to hearing from you.

Sincerely,

Maria S. Perez

Kathy Avila

138 Oceanview Drive / Honolulu, HI 96822
(808) 555-1196

May 15, 20__

Joseph Leathers, Executive Director
East-West Galleries
14 Reed Circle
Honolulu, HI 96822

Dear Mr. Leathers:

The enclosed resume is submitted in application for the position of Assistant Curator announced May 12. I would appreciate being considered for the position.

I feel that my substantial experience in museum management and fine arts programming has prepared me well for the types of duties mentioned in the job description. As you will see, the responsibilities I fulfilled while serving at the San Diego Arts Center were very similar to those required by this position.

I would be interested in meeting with you in person to discuss the position requirements and how I might address them. I would also be eager to provide letters of recommendation or any other details you might request.

Thank you very much for your consideration. I admire the outstanding image your galleries have developed, and I hope that I can become a part of your organization.

You can reach me at any time by calling the number listed above. I will look forward to hearing from you.

Yours truly,

Kathy Avila

∽ Kathy Avila ∽
138 Oceanview Drive
Honolulu, HI 96822
(808) 555-1196

May 15, 20__

Joseph Leathers, Executive Director
East-West Galleries
14 Reed Circle
Honolulu, HI 96822

Dear Mr. Leathers:

I suppose everyone would like to live in Hawaii, and I'm no exception. Are you getting many applications from places like Alaska or northern Canada?

Geography aside, I am very interested in being considered for the position of Assistant Curator announced May 12.

What do I have to offer? Here are two points to consider.

First, my substantial experience in museum management and fine arts programming has prepared me well for the types of duties described in the job announcement. As you will see, the responsibilities I fulfilled while serving at the San Diego Arts Center were very similar to those expected of this position.

Second, I am highly familiar with both Asian and American art, as evidenced by my academic background and record of scholarly publications. Thus a position where East meets West would seem a real natural for me.

My resume (enclosed) provides a sketch of my background and experience. If you would like more details, please contact me.

Thank you very much for your consideration. I admire the outstanding image your galleries have developed, and I hope that I can become a part of your organization.

Yours truly,

Kathy Avila

MARTHA HAVELIN
311 Cobalt Road
Verona, PA 15147
(412) 555-0608
marhav333@xxx.com

January 12, 20__

Dr. Joanne Galloway, Director of Research
Ekton Biotechnology
16 East Industrial Park
Willingboro, NJ 08406

Dear Dr. Galloway:

I was given your name by your former colleague at Ekton, Dr. David Posey. He indicated that you are planning to expand your technical staff and suggested that I contact you. Thus I am sending the enclosed resume.

I have had a great deal of experience in performing a variety of laboratory support tasks. While serving as a laboratory technician at Eastern Labs, I have refined skills originally gained through my studies at Westchester State University, where I also served as a laboratory assistant for Dr. Poteet. This training and experience has prepared me well for a wide range of laboratory responsibilities.

I have excellent research skills and thorough work habits. Performance evaluations (summaries available) have indicated that I am a highly motivated and dedicated worker.

The enclosed resume provides more details about my background. If you would like more information, please contact me. I would be delighted to meet with you to discuss my qualifications in further detail.

Thank you for your consideration.

Sincerely,

Marthy Havelin

MARTHA HAVELIN

311 Cobalt Road
Verona, PA 15147
(412) 555-0608
marhav333@xxx.com

January 12, 20__

Dr. Joanne Galloway, Director of Research
Ekton Biotechnology
16 East Industrial Park
Willingboro, NJ 08406

Dear Dr. Galloway:

Could your staff benefit by adding an experienced laboratory technician? If so, the enclosed resume may be of interest.

I was given your name by your former colleague at Ekton, Dr. David Posey. He indicated that you are planning to expand your technical staff and suggested that I contact you.

I've had a great deal of experience in performing a variety of laboratory support tasks. While serving as a lab technician at Eastern Labs, I have refined skills originally gained through my studies at Westchester State University, where I also served as a laboratory assistant for Dr. Poteet. This training and experience have prepared me well for a wide range of responsibilities.

I have excellent research skills and thorough work habits. Performance evaluations (summaries available) have indicated that I am a highly motivated and dedicated worker.

If after reviewing my resume you desire more information, please contact me. I'd be delighted to meet with you to discuss my qualifications in further detail.

Thanks for your consideration.

Sincerely,

Martha Havelin

Tessa Boyd

P.O. Box 9188 / Kansas City, MO 64117
(816) 555-4099 / boydtr@xxx.com

June 22, 20__

Mr. Daniel Glisson
The Hagan Corporation
410 E. 10th Street
Kansas City, MO 64116-4302

Dear Mr. Glisson:

Please accept this letter and the enclosed resume in application for the position of Assistant Director of Security currently being advertised by your company.

My background in security work, originating in military training and experience and strengthened through my recent work in the private sector, has provided me with a firm foundation in performing a variety of security-related tasks. I am experienced in supervising others as well as working independently to maintain a high level of security.

I would appreciate your reviewing the enclosed resume, which outlines my background in more detail. Please let me know if I can become a part of your company's future.

I will be glad to meet with you at any time to discuss employment possibilities with your firm.

Thank you for your consideration.

Sincerely yours,

Tessa Boyd

❖ Tessa Boyd ❖
P.O. Box 9188
Kansas City, MO 64117
(816) 555-4099
boydtr@xxx.com

June 22, 20__

Mr. Daniel Glisson
The Hagan Corporation
410 E. 10th Street
Kansas City, MO 64116-4302

Dear Mr. Glisson:

What would you do if a security crisis developed at your company, and your Director of Security was out of town? If I were the Assistant Director, you could turn to me with confidence.

I'd like the chance to prove the veracity of this statement. Please consider me for the position of Assistant Director of Security, as recently advertised.

My background in security work originated in military training and experience and then was strengthened through work in the private sector. This combined experience has provided me with a firm foundation in performing a variety of security-related tasks. I am experienced in supervising others as well as working independently to maintain a high level of security.

Please review the enclosed resume, which outlines my background in more detail, and let me know if I can become a part of your company's future. I'll be glad to meet with you at any time to discuss employment possibilities with your firm.

Thank you for your consideration.

Sincerely yours,

Tessa Boyd

LESLIE GOLDBERG
41 Liberty Avenue, Apartment 12B
Monaca, PA 15061
(412) 555-2877
goldstar@xxx.net

December 3, 20__

Mr. Ryan S. Adams, Assistant Director
General Equipment Corporation
P.O. Box 7271
Erie, PA 16505

Dear Mr. Adams:

Thank you for sending me information about your company.

Enclosed is a copy of my resume. As you will note, I have a strong background in office equipment sales. Should I join your company, I could bring a fresh perspective to your operations and help in your quest to make your office equipment division a more integral part of General Equipment Corporation.

I was especially interested to learn of your plans to expand your business internationally. My previous experience in England and Northern Ireland should prove helpful in this regard.

My resume provides additional important details. After you have reviewed it, please let me know if you would like to discuss the present or future needs of your firm, and how I might meet them.

Yours truly,

Leslie Goldberg

LESLIE GOLDBERG

41 Liberty Avenue, Apartment 12B
Monaca, PA 15061
(412) 555-2877
goldstar@xxx.net

December 3, 20__

Mr. Ryan S. Adams, Assistant Director
General Equipment Corporation
P.O. Box 7271
Erie, PA 16505

Dear Mr. Adams:

Do you have good contacts in the United Kingdom? I do. My international experience is just one reason you should consider me for a position with your company.

Most importantly, my background in office equipment sales could prove a significant asset should I join your company. I could bring a fresh perspective to your operations and help in your quest to make your office equipment division a more integral part of General Equipment Corporation.

I was especially interested to learn of your plans to expand your business internationally. My previous experience in England and Northern Ireland should prove helpful in this regard.

The enclosed resume provides additional details about my qualifications. After you have reviewed it, please let me know if you would like to discuss the present or future needs of your firm, and how I might meet them.

Yours truly,

Leslie Goldberg

JANET BRYNER

108 Bloom Street / Ottawa, ON K2C 4A4 Canada
(604) 555-4865 / E-mail: bryner@xxx.com

March 16, 20__

Pat M. Hanks
Futures, Inc.
1084 Lake City Way, SE
Seattle, WA 98125

Dear Pat Hanks:

This letter and the enclosed resume are submitted in response to your recent advertisement for a Director of Facilities.

I have a solid background in facilities management through my service with United Enterprises, where I currently supervise custodial and maintenance operations for a six-building complex. I am skilled in personnel supervision, construction planning, preventive maintenance, and the use of new technologies such as computerized energy management.

My resume provides basic details regarding my background and experience; if additional details are needed, please contact me. I would be glad to meet with you in person at any time.

Thank you for considering my application. I would appreciate hearing from you.

Yours truly,

Janet Bryner

JANET BRYNER
108 Bloom Street
Ottawa, ON K2C 4A4 Canada
(604) 555-4865
E-mail: bryner@xxx.com

March 16, 20__

Pat M. Hanks
Futures, Inc.
1084 Lake City Way, SE
Seattle, WA 98125

Dear Pat Hanks:

Where I work, you could eat off the floor. Literally.

Of course, I realize you probably don't *want* to dine from the floor. But I believe in keeping facilities as clean as possible, and ours are spotless.

The same would be true at your company if I were your Director of Facilities. As you might guess, I would like to apply for this position in response to your recent advertisement. A copy of my resume is enclosed.

I have a solid background in facilities management through my service with United Enterprises, where I currently supervise custodial and maintenance operations for a six-building complex. I'm skilled in personnel supervision, construction planning, preventive maintenance, and the use of new technologies such as computerized energy management.

My resume provides basic details regarding my background and experience. If additional details are needed, please contact me. I would be glad to meet with you in person at any time.

Thanks for considering my application. I'll appreciate hearing from you.

Yours truly,

Janet Bryner

BECKY RAUGH
301 Anderson Avenue
Franklin Park, IL 60131
(847) 555-7160
raugh123@xxx.net

October 23, 20__

Alvin E. Lewis, General Manager
InfoMix Corporation
P.O. Box 494
Janesville, WI 53547

Dear Mr. Lewis:

I would like to apply for the position of Staff Photographer with your company as advertised in the October 22 edition of the *Daily Gazette*. Enclosed are a resume and samples of my work.

I have just earned a bachelor's degree from the Illinois School of Art and Design, with a major in photography and a minor in graphic design. I also served as a part-time staff photographer in the school's public relations office. During this time my photos received a great deal of acclaim from professors and supervisors.

Please let me know if you would like to see additional examples of my work. I would also be willing to take on a sample assignment so that you can judge not only my abilities as a photographer, but also my resourcefulness in completing assignments. Of course, I would also appreciate an opportunity to meet with you in person and discuss the position more fully.

If I can provide additional information, please contact me. I look forward to hearing from you.

Yours sincerely,

Becky Raugh

BECKY RAUGH

301 Anderson Avenue
Franklin Park, IL 60131
(847) 555-7160
raugh123@xxx.net

October 23, 20__

Alvin E. Lewis, General Manager
InfoMix Corporation
P.O. Box 494
Janesville, WI 53547

Dear Mr. Lewis:

Smile! No, I'm not about to take your photo, although that could be arranged. But if I were Staff Photographer at your company, smiles would be common, at least in response to my work.

I would love a chance to back up this statement. So please consider me for the position advertised in the October 22 edition of the *Daily Gazette*. Enclosed are a resume and samples of my work.

I have just earned a bachelor's degree from the Illinois School of Art and Design, with a major in photography and a minor in graphic design. I also served as a part-time staff photographer in the school's public relations office. During this time my photos received a great deal of acclaim from professors and supervisors.

Please let me know if you would like to see additional examples of my work. I would also be willing to take on a sample assignment so that you can judge not only my abilities as a photographer, but also my resourcefulness in completing assignments. Of course, I'd also appreciate an opportunity to meet with you in person and discuss the position more fully.

If I can provide additional information, please contact me. I look forward to hearing from you.

Yours sincerely,

Becky Raugh

Jason Helms

405 Moore Street / Baraboo, WI 53547
(608) 555-2628 / helmsmen@xxxxx.net

May 31, 20__

Dan Salerno, Personnel Manager
Cox Instrumentation
P.O. Box 774
Baraboo, WI 53547

Dear Mr. Salerno:

I am writing to inquire about employment opportunities with Cox Instrumentation.
Enclosed is a resume outlining my experience.

As you will note, I have solid experience in maintaining and repairing various types of
instruments. I have served for two years as an instrumentation technician in the chemical
industry, during which time I have proved myself a highly reliable worker. I have a strong
work ethic and a penchant for accuracy and attention to detail.

My current objective is a position in instrumentation with a leading company such as
your own. I would be grateful if you would consider me for any position openings, either
now or in the near future.

I would be happy to meet with you at your convenience. I would also be glad to provide
letters of recommendation or other information.

Thanks for your consideration. I hope to hear from you soon.

Sincerely yours,

Jason Helms

❧ Jason Helms ❧

405 Moore Street
Baraboo, WI 53547
(608) 555-2628
helmsmen@xxxxx.net

May 31, 20__

Dan Salerno, Personnel Manager
Cox Instrumentation
P.O. Box 774
Baraboo, WI 53547

Dear Mr. Salerno:

I keep watching the newspapers, but I have yet to see any ads announcing vacancies with your company. So I can't wait any longer. Here is a copy of my resume. I offer this on the chance that now or in the near future, you may be interested in adding to your staff of instrumentation technicians.

As you will note, I have solid experience in maintaining and repairing various types of instruments. I have served for two years as an instrumentation technician in the chemical industry, during which time I have proved myself a highly reliable worker. I have a strong work ethic and a penchant for accuracy.

My goal is a technical position with a leading company such as your own. I would be grateful if you would consider me for any openings that may develop.

I would be happy to meet with you at your convenience. I'd also be glad to provide letters of recommendation or other information.

Thanks for your consideration. I hope to hear from you soon.

Sincerely yours,

Jason Helms

DOUGLAS RIDPATH
2134 Lakeview Drive
Duluth, GA 30155
(770) 555-2781

August 9, 20__

Ted Casey, President
MMB Tech Systems
870 W. Tipton Street
Huntington, IN 46750

Dear Mr. Casey:

I am submitting the enclosed resume for your consideration in the event that you need to add to your sales staff. As a highly experienced sales professional, I would be available should you wish to add a dependable employee to your company.

As my resume shows, my experience over the past eight years has prepared me well to perform a wide variety of sales and marketing functions. I am skilled in adjusting to different situations and flexibly addressing the needs of both existing and new customers.

I am energetic, highly motivated, and dependable. I take great pride in performing high-quality work, and have been recognized through a number of awards (see resume) as a sales professional with skills that are well above average.

I would appreciate the opportunity to meet with you in person to discuss your company's needs and how I might meet them. If you would like letters of recommendation or any other details, I would be glad to provide them.

Please let me know if there is a possibility of my joining your company. Thank you for your consideration.

Yours truly,

Douglas Ridpath

DOUGLAS RIDPATH

2134 Lakeview Drive
Duluth, GA 30155
(770) 555-2781

August 9, 20__

Ted Casey, President
MMB Tech Systems
870 W. Tipton Street
Huntington, IN 46750

Dear Mr. Casey:

How would you like to hire an award-winning sales professional who can guarantee stellar results? OK, I know I can't offer your money back if you hire me and then find my performance lacking. But if I become an MMB representative, you *will* be satisfied.

This is not empty rhetoric. In each year of my career, I have set sales records and earned rave reviews from supervisors, peers, and clients. As my resume shows, my experience over the past eight years has prepared me well to perform a wide variety of sales and marketing functions. I am skilled in adjusting to different situations and flexibly addressing the needs of both existing and new customers.

I am energetic, highly motivated, and dependable. I take great pride in performing high-quality work, and have been recognized through a number of awards (see resume) as a sales professional with skills that are well above average.

I would appreciate the opportunity to meet with you in person to discuss your company's needs and how I might meet them. If you would like letters of recommendation or any other details, I would be glad to provide them.

Please let me know if there is a possibility of my joining your company. Thank you for your consideration.

Yours truly,

Douglas Ridpath

4
Playing the Cover Letter Game

Applying for a job is somewhat like playing a game. Sometimes you win, and sometimes you don't. In many instances the odds are against you. You might be applying for a job even though no openings have been announced, just on the chance that something might develop. Or you might be responding to an advertisement along with scores or hundreds of others who want the same job.

At the same time, it only takes one success for you to obtain a good job. So despite all the hassles involved, it's worth playing the game.

Within this context, here are four basic approaches to seeking jobs.

1. **The shot in the dark.** Here, you send a letter and resume on the chance that an employer might be considering adding new employees, even though no current openings exist in your area of interest. Part of this thinking is that you might position yourself for consideration for the future, even if an opening is not immediately forthcoming.

2. **Follow-up on an earlier contact.** This is not unlike a shot in the dark, but with the advantage that you are reminding an employer about your interest instead of venturing it for the first time. If employers have suggested that you contact them at a later date, and that date has now arrived, this can be a great way to get started.

3. **Third-party reference.** If a colleague, friend, or other person familiar with an employer suggests that you initiate a contact, you can use this as a valid reason for sending a letter and resume. A third-party reference might or might not carry weight with any given employer, but at worst it

provides you with an excuse to call attention to your credentials. At best, it might provide an inside advantage for further consideration.

4. **Response to an ad or notice of vacancy.** In some ways, this is the best situation for an aggressive job seeker. With a job announcement you know that an opening exists, and you generally have access to details about qualities or credentials the employer desires. This in turn allows you to shape your letter and other application materials around these expressed preferences. The negative side is that others who read the same ad have the same opportunity, but at least you're operating from a common knowledge base.

You might take any or all of these approaches to seeking jobs. In making application plans, consider which approach offers the most potential for each employer, and then prepare correspondence accordingly.

APPLICATION COMPONENTS

The typical job application consists of a resume and a cover letter. But employers might require you to submit other materials as part of the application process. This depends on the policies of individual employers, and it also varies widely from one type of work to another. For example, for professions involving writing, art production, or photography, employers might ask that you submit samples of your work.

Depending on the circumstances, employers might ask you to submit materials such as the following:

- A completed application form (preprinted form provided by the employer) *instead* of a resume
- A completed application form to which a resume may be attached
- Letters of recommendation sent on your behalf by others
- Copies of letters of recommendation, written by others but assembled and submitted by you
- College or trade school transcripts
- Copies of diplomas
- Proof of certification or licensure
- Samples of your work

Increasingly, employers are expecting that resumes and cover letters (or their equivalent) be submitted electronically. But the same basic principles apply.

Questions to Ask Before Writing a Cover Letter

- To whom should it be addressed?
- Will it be transmitted by mail, or submitted electronically? If the latter, how should I adapt the format?
- Do I have the exact information for the designated recipient (correct spelling of names, precise wording of position title, etc.)?
- How can I individualize *this* letter for *this* position/employer?
- What strengths should I note?

- Should I amplify information provided in my resume? If so, which details would make the greatest positive impact without duplicating information?
- What information can I provide that is not included in my resume?
- How can I make my letter stand out from others of the same type?

INCLUDING EXTRA TIDBITS

Cover letters are especially valuable when they add an extra bit of information not contained in your resume. You might emphasize a specific qualification, highlight a relevant experience, or otherwise provide a key detail you'd like to call to the attention of a prospective employer. Often such an addition will apply only to one employer, and thus help individualize your letter. For example, it might respond to information contained in an advertisement.

Here are some examples of tidbits you can add to letters:

- *Ad content*: "Several positions are open with the corporation, some at branch offices located around the country."
  - *Cover letter tidbit*: Your letter includes a comment that you would like to be considered for all positions, regardless of location.
  - *Alternative:* Your letter includes a sentence explaining that you wish to be considered only for positions in a particular area.
- *Ad content*: "Persons with disabilities are encouraged to apply."
  - *Cover letter tidbit:* You include a sentence noting that you have a disability (for example, that you must use a wheelchair) and that you are especially interested in companies such as this one with a strong record of hiring people with disabilities.

Along with the ability to focus on needs expressed in advertisements, cover letters also allow you to add information about yourself that would not normally be included in a resume. For example, you might note time or scheduling restrictions.

- *Fact:* You will be traveling on a long-planned vacation to Scotland for a three-week period.
  - *Cover letter tidbit*: You add the following sentence: "Please note that I will be out of the country May 5-27. I will be happy to meet with you at your convenience either before this time or immediately after."
- *Fact:* You are unable to work daytime hours during the week.
  - *Cover letter tidbit:* You add a sentence explaining that you are a student during the day but are available during evenings and weekends.

THE MATTER OF DATES

Every business letter, cover letters included, should include the date you send it.

If you don't use letterhead stationery (or simulate the traditional appearance of letterhead with your computer), place the date in the last line of the inside address, as in the following example:

KATHY DANACZKO
1902 E. Golf Road
Cleveland, OH 44145
(216) 555-8831
March 12, 2004

With letterhead stationery (or simulated letterhead), the date can be centered at the top underneath your name and address.

Please note that the sample letters provided in this book *do not have complete dates* because they are offered as examples that can be used over time and will not become outdated anytime soon. But in developing your own letters, don't forget to include the date.

Also, when revising a copy of a previously used letter that has been stored electronically, don't forget to change the date. This is a common error too often made by people who take advantage of material that has been stored electronically.

DON'T BE ANNOYING

Writing a slam dunk cover letter takes effort. But don't be guilty of trying *too* hard. Otherwise, you could end up annoying prospective employers instead of impressing them.

As a comparison, think of the hard-to-like person who tries to insert himself into every conversation. You know the type: he tells jokes and then laughs louder than anyone else, dominates every conversation, and eventually causes people to avoid him. You don't want your letters to have a similar effect.

On the other hand, evidence of not trying hard enough can also be annoying. An obvious lack of effort makes it appear you don't care enough about getting a job to put forth your best work. It also creates doubt about the type of worker you would turn out to be.

Either way, it pays to avoid anything that might annoy a potential employer. Here are some examples.

1. **Sloppiness.** Nobody is impressed by sloppy work, and some people are downright offended by it. Be sure to avoid all of the following:

   ■ Handwritten letters. These are a definite no-no in today's business world, with the possible exception of personalized thank-you notes.

   ■ Narrow margins. Margins of less than one inch make letters look too cramped. Be sure to leave plenty of white space, especially with short letters.

   ■ Spacing problems. Extra spaces between words or letters, inconsistent margins or indentations, and other spacing problems can make an otherwise effective letter look like the work of an amateur.

2. **Extra punctuation.** An exclamation point here and there is OK, but one or two is the limit in a single letter. Otherwise, it's as though you're shouting at the reader, "Hey, look, this is important!" Also, never use a series of exclamation points or question marks at the end of a sentence; that smacks of middle school students passing notes in class.

3. **Excessive use of attention-getters.** Avoid all of these:
   - Spelling out words in all uppercase letters just to focus attention on key points
   - Excessive use of boldface type or different fonts within the same letter
   - Frequent underlining of important words or phrases
   - Use of any color of ink other than black

4. **Hyperbole.** You won't win points by exaggerating. Don't say that a company will make the biggest mistake it has ever made if you're not hired. Don't claim you're *the* best person in North America at doing your job (even if you consider that the truth). Describe your strong points, but don't lay it on too thick. One good way to avoid hyperbole is to use qualifying words and phrases such as "one of the best" or "perhaps the single most successful."

5. **Undue urgency.** Even if you're desperate for a job, you can't demand an immediate response to your letter. Similarly, it's not appropriate to place a deadline on your interest (for example, don't say you need a quick response because you're considering another job offer). The employer is the one with the prerogative for setting deadlines, not an applicant at the early stages of the application process.

6. **Improper language.** Curse words (even mild usage, as in "I've been called the best damn salesman in the company's history") are always inappropriate, even if you're trying to be humorous. The same is true of sexist language or any words or phrases that might offend a particular group of people.

7. **Overly long sentences.** A letter of application should be concise and easy to read. A series of long, complex sentences stands a good chance of annoying the reader.

FIVE STEPS FOR SAVING TIME IN COMPOSING COVER LETTERS

When you embark on a job search, you are instantly busy. Use these steps to help you use your time as efficiently as possible.

1. Develop a draft letter and review it carefully.
2. Store the letter electronically (including at least one backup copy on a second computer, or on a floppy disk, CD, or removeable storage device).
3. Use the same basic letter repeatedly, changing names and addresses of recipients.
4. In redoing each electronic version of your letter, be careful to remove all traces of the previous recipient. Don't forget to change the date and salutation, as well as the inside address. Be sure to proofread carefully.
5. As time permits, vary the letter's main message so that you have several versions of differing length and content. Then you can choose from this selection whenever a new cover letter is needed.

THE HUMOR FACTOR

When should you use humor in cover letters? The answer is almost never.

Here are some good things that could happen if you make humorous remarks:

- The reader could smile.
- The reader could laugh.
- The reader could be favorably impressed by your personality and thus more likely to invite you for an interview.
- Your sparkling humor could grab the attention of an initial reader, who might pass it on to a friend in Hollywood, and before you know it you've been hired as a network comedy writer! (Dream on. . . .)

Things that could go wrong include:

- The reader will recognize your attempt at humor and think it mildly funny but inappropriate for a job-related letter.
- The reader will notice your stab at humor but will not find it funny and will form a negative impression as a result.
- Not only will the reader think the remark unfunny, but he or she might seriously question your suitability for the job for which you are applying.
- The reader will deem your humorous remarks tasteless and eliminate you from further consideration for employment.

All because you tried to be funny!

The bottom line is this: Don't use humor in cover letters unless you have a truly compelling reason to do so. Examples of compelling reasons might include: you're applying for a job as a comedian; the ad specifies a good sense of humor as a job requirement; or you're writing to a close friend who just happens to have a job opening, and who thinks your sense of humor is your best quality. Otherwise, do not include humorous remarks in cover letters.

Does this mean abandoning humor and becoming a faceless cog in the wheels of commerce? No, it just means waiting until an appropriate time. The truth is, written humor is difficult to convey well. You might hit your mark, but then again you might miss it completely. And because you're not physically present with the reader, you might never know whether it was effective.

Oral person-to-person humor is a different matter. In interacting with others, even in situations as formal as job interviews, the use of humor might be OK. You'll generally know when this is the case because others will be joking or laughing, and if you're socially astute you can read the situation and react accordingly. (Even here, it might be best to go easy on humor, because one inappropriate remark can be highly damaging.)

MAKING BEST USE OF E-MAIL AND INTERNET OPTIONS

As previously noted, a reality of twenty-first century life is that more and more business is being conducted via electronic mail as opposed to what some now call snail mail, or ordinary mail service. With the explosive growth of the Internet and various online services, increasing numbers of businesses, as well as individuals, have made this a standard communication medium.

As Internet use becomes more common, possibilities for sending correspondence electronically or posting information on Web sites continue to grow. In developing cover letters, keep these points in mind:

1. If you have an e-mail address, list it on your cover letter along with your mailing address and telephone number. This will allow employers to contact you quickly if they choose. It might also have the benefit of hinting that you are computer proficient (or at least show that because you are online, you obviously know how to operate a computer, process e-mail, and so forth).

2. Do not use e-mail to submit an application letter (or other type of letter) unless the employer has specifically stated that electronic submissions are welcomed. If this is the case, it will normally be stated in classified ads or printed job announcements. Some bad things can happen if you violate this practice:

   ■ The employer might not accept applications submitted electronically, and thus you will not be considered for employment.

   ■ Even if an employer accepts an electronic message in lieu of correspondence sent by mail, your application might suffer in comparison to others when it comes to appearance. An e-mail message might lack the crisp, attractive look of a carefully word-processed letter.

   ■ If you are sure e-mail messages are acceptable, make certain to follow the same standards of excellence you would apply in a traditional letter. While electronic mail usually has a less formal tone and approach than regular business correspondence, this more casual approach might not be suitable for cover letters accompanying resumes or job applications. One challenge with electronic communications is that it is now so commonplace to communicate with e-mail that it's easy to forget about tone, sentence structure, and letter format.

"Candidates beware," says Lena Bottos of Salary.com.

E-mail tends to be used as a casual form of communication. Don't fall into that trap. Many people, especially younger people who have grown up in the e-mail and instant messaging world, have to be reminded that there are rules for grammar, punctuation, capitalization, and style. Even with an e-mail cover letter, you must use them. Period.

SPECIAL E-MAIL TIPS

Career expert Kevin Donlin offers these tips on adapting the use of cover letters to an e-mail format.

   ■ For best results, send your cover letter (and resume) both inside your e-mail and also as an attachment. That way, even if you're using Word-Perfect and the employer is using Word, for example, you're sure that your documents can be read.

   ■ Copy and paste the text of your cover letter into the body of an e-mail, along with your resume (cover letter first, resume second);

- Attach the document (in Word or WordPerfect) to the e-mail;
- Send a test message to yourself and a friend to see how the whole thing will look and print—if it's a mess, adjust and test until it works.

POSTING ON JOB WEB SITES

John Haynes, an experienced human resources professional and career search expert, says that if a job Web site allows the option of posting cover letters, be sure to take this opportunity.

"It is a great introduction," he says, "and can further speak to specific accomplishments and skills that you might opt not to cover in your resume, or due to resume length might not fit into your resume."

He adds that for those attempting to make the transition from a non-managerial role to one that is managerial, a cover letter might be the difference.

"Writing skills are highly important in management positions, especially in drafting reports, presentations, and communicating information to staff, upper management, and clients," Haynes says. "I cannot stress the fact enough that the cover letter might be an indicator of the level of your writing skills."

Salary.com's Lena Bottos adds these tips for posting cover letters, or the equivalent information, on job Web sites:

- Job posting sites will most likely require you to have a text version of your resume. This means that the first version seen will not translate well when printed out. Be sure to follow up with a formatted version. If the Web site allows you to preview what a potential employer will see, take the time to look and then modify your format to make sure it is as easy to read as possible. This will help your cover letter and resume get the careful review they deserve.

- Because many people now use job boards as a means to get their resume in front of potential employers, it is easy to skip the step of writing a cover letter. This is unfortunate because a cover letter is a great first chance to put a personality with a resume. So when your are contacted after someone has seen your resume on a job board, it is best to follow up with an e-mail that is a cover letter and has attached a formatted, print-ready version of your resume.

SOURCES OF HELP IN WRITING COVER LETTERS

When you sit down to write a cover letter, keep in mind that you're not working in a vacuum. If you encounter a problem or simply need some help in doing the best possible job, take advantage of some of the many resources available to you.

Reference Books on Writing

If you're unsure about some point of grammar or punctuation, don't guess! Instead, consult a book such as the *Harbrace College Handbook* (see the list of resources provided in Appendix A). Such books are designed as references to provide answers about grammar, usage, and other elements of written communication. For example, say you're not sure whether to use *who* or *whom*.

Just look up *Who vs. Whom* in the index, turn to the appropriate page, and you'll find a summary of the basic rules regarding use of these words, including several helpful examples.

Be sure you own at least one reference book on grammar, usage, or writing. Keep it at hand when writing cover letters—and any other documents, for that matter.

Spell-Check Programs

If you work at a computer (and who doesn't these days?), a truly helpful feature is the spell-check function included in any good word-processing or e-mail program. With a minimum of effort, you can assure yourself that words are spelled properly (after all, the computer does the real work here). Before printing and signing a letter, make certain you have spell-checked it. Then proofread it for grammatical errors, misplaced words, etc. A word of caution, though: do not rely too heavily on spell-check functions. While helpful, they are far from foolproof. After running such programs to catch glaring errors, be sure to review the material carefully to make sure no mistakes remain.

Thesaurus

Coming up with just the right word can be difficult. Varying your vocabulary can also be a challenge, but effective writing demands that you demonstrate at least some variety in word choice. A good thesaurus can be extremely helpful here. For this purpose, consider buying your own copy of a standard such as *Roget's International Thesaurus*. Thesaurus programs provided in word-processing software can also be helpful.

Peer Editor

Have a friend or relative with good writing or editorial skills? If so, ask her or him to take a look at a sample letter and suggest improvements. It never hurts to get someone else's viewpoint. Of course, you should be the final arbiter if there is any disagreement. But an objective reader might detect an error or flaw that you overlooked.

OTHER TYPES OF LETTERS

The discussion in this book focuses on cover letters used in conjunction with resumes. But keep in mind that other types of letters might also be important in the job-search process.

Other Cover Letters

Not all letters prepared by job applicants relate to resumes. For example, you might want to follow up on an interview by thanking the employer for giving you the opportunity to discuss employment possibilities. Or you might combine this with a message about the submission of related documents. For instance, many employers will reimburse job applicants for travel costs involved in coming for an interview. This normally happens some time after the interview has taken place because you don't know how much expenses have totaled until that time. To obtain reimbursement, you might need to send documentation of expenses to the employer. A cover letter will be in order here, and you might use it to add an expression of thanks.

Cover letters of this type might be needed for such items as documents stating credentials or certification. Or they might deal with an item of special interest to the employer discussed during the interview (for example, a report you have written that directly relates to a problem the employer is facing at her company).

The most important quality of such letters is brevity. They should be short and to the point. This is not the place to tout your capabilities or convince an employer to hire you; hiring decisions at this juncture will be based on your interview and other information. In this case, a letter should simply state what you are enclosing, without a great deal of elaboration. An exception would be a note of thanks at the end of the letter. But the main purpose of this type of letter is a simple transaction—in essence, a note that states, "Here is the information you need."

Stand-Alone Letters

In addition to these types of cover letters, other types of letters have their place in the job application process. While not strictly cover letters (because they stand on their own instead of accompanying other materials), they are nevertheless worth noting here.

Before the Interview

- A request for information about the job
- A request for information about the employer, such as an annual report or catalog of products
- A request for information about job application procedures

After the Interview

- A thank-you letter
- A request for follow-up information
- A letter withdrawing your name from consideration for employment

As with cover letters, it is important that these types of letters be neat, concise, and error-free. Most such letters will be very brief and matter-of-fact in approach and content. Otherwise, the same principles of good writing apply here as with other correspondence.

SUBMISSION MECHANICS

Once you have written and rewritten a cover letter and polished your resume, you are ready to apply for that once-in-a-lifetime job. When you have identified one or more possible employers and are ready to mail your application materials or submit them electronically, follow these submission guidelines.

- Double-check spelling of names. This applies to the names of companies as well as those of individual managers.
- Make sure e-mail addresses are correct. A message that bounces back just wastes time.
- If you're using traditional mail, do not staple the cover letter to the resume. The letter should stand apart as an introduction to the resume. Also, be sure the return address is included on both the letter and the envelope.

COVER LETTER CHECKLIST

Use this checklist as an outline for developing your own cover letters. In Column 1, check off details that are not likely to change from one cover letter to the next. In Column 2, check information that will vary in letters sent to different employers. Make sure each item is included in each letter for which it is applicable.

Column 1	*Column 2*
Your name.	Today's date.
Your address.	Company address.
Your telephone number.	Name of recipient.
Your fax number (if applicable).	Title of recipient.
Your e-mail address.	Comment(s) on why
	you are a strong job
Salutation.	candidate.
Reference to the job in which	Reference to personal
you're interested.	connection (if applicable).
Statement that your resume	Clever hook or opening
is enclosed.	statement (optional).
Reminder of availability	
for interview.	
Closing.	
Signature.	
Notations (if applicable).	

ADDRESSING WEAKNESSES

The job application process is all about *strengths*. As a job applicant, you focus on your strengths as they apply to a job in which you're interested.

But what about weaknesses? Everyone has them. The question is how to deal with your own weaknesses when pursuing a job. One traditional approach is to ignore them. You focus on your strengths, and hope that a potential employer won't notice any major weaknesses related to the job. It's like discovering you have a rip in the seat of your pants. If you're not in a position to change clothes or repair the tear, you just smile and hope no one will notice!

A different approach is to meet potential problems head-on. You do this by addressing them yourself instead of hoping they will not come up. True, this alternative doesn't always work (but then neither does smiling your way past your ripped pants). The head-on approach does, on the other hand, allow you to frame things in your own terms and explain situations that could damage your chances of landing a job.

Here are some examples of ways to use cover letters to address weaknesses or potential problems that might show up in the material presented in your resume.

Problem/Weakness: You lack experience.

Evidence: Your resume shows limited experience in terms of paid employment.

Action: Emphasize in your cover letter factors that might offset (at least in part) a lack of paid work experience, such as:

- Internships
- Volunteer work
- Formal academic training
- Attendance at seminars or workshops
- A strong work ethic as evidenced by exceptional accomplishments requiring hard work (for example, running in marathon races)

Problem/Weakness: You have work experience, but it's not directly related to this potential job.

Evidence: Your resume lists jobs you have held, but they are not in the same field as the job you're seeking.

Action: In your cover letter, you focus on traits you have developed rather than specific tasks you have completed for other jobs.

Problem/Weakness: You lost your last job as a result of downsizing.

Evidence: Your resume makes it clear you are not presently employed.

Action: In your cover letter, you admit that you were a victim of recent downsizing, but note that it was your company's financial situation, not your own shortcomings, that was the real culprit. You back this up by citing strong references, recognition you have received, or other evidence of competence. (Note: some people recommend against calling attention to this factor, so it would fall somewhere in the Bold and Brassy category.)

The main requirement is to be positive. If you decide to address weaknesses, don't dwell on them. Don't get defensive. Just use such references as a bridge to statements about your competence.

WRITING RESUMES

A cover letter is not much good without a resume or other enclosure. Otherwise, what's the point? So be sure to put in as much thought and effort on assembling a great resume as you do in writing top-notch cover letters.

For best results in this area, consult helpful resources such as *Slam Dunk Resumes* (see the list of resources in Appendix A). Also, keep in mind the following tips.

Material presented in resumes and cover letters should be both consistent and complementary. Double-check all facts to make certain that they are accurate and do not contradict one another. At the same time, use cover letters to highlight or add to information presented in your resume. By their very nature as concise introductions to you and your qualifications, letters cannot repeat all the details listed in a resume. So when writing letters, choose examples carefully.

Resumes should always be current. Don't bother to send a resume that is not 100-percent up-to-date. It's a good idea to keep a resume file and use it to add new details as they develop. Then periodically update the resume itself. With the use of a computer, this is a relatively easy task.

Resumes should be neat. Just as with cover letters, resumes create strong first impressions. Never make do with a sloppy resume. Instead, make sure it is well organized and neatly presented. It need not make use of fancy fonts or graphics, but neatness is a must.

Use resumes as resource material for your cover letters. Most people develop the resume first, and then turn to cover letters when they're ready to apply for a job. Before starting a cover letter, read over your resume and consider which points would best be emphasized in an accompanying letter.

5

Using Cover Letters to Best Advantage

WHERE DO WE GO FROM HERE?

When an NBA all-star makes the winning dunk at the end of a hard-fought game, it is a glorious moment. The crowd cheers, teammates slap him on the back, and sports editors make sure they have a tape to show on the late news.

But as the excitement of the moment fades, the game goes on. And after that game comes another.

Once you write a successful cover letter, your situation is similar to that of the basketball player who has slammed it in for two. There is still more work to be done.

MEASURING SUCCESS

An important step after you have submitted one or more cover letters is to measure their success. Just how do you gauge the success of such a letter? That can be complicated.

Ultimately, you might say, a good cover letter will lead to a new job. But using this as a standard is not really fair. After all, cover letters (and resumes) rarely provoke an employer to hire someone based on written materials alone. More typically, they lead to *interviews*. Once you're granted an interview, that becomes the opportunity to convince a prospective employer that you're the right choice.

As one measure of success, ask yourself if you are getting interviews. If your letters and resumes are resulting in job interviews, something must be right about the written materials you are developing.

If you're *not* landing interviews, does that mean your cover letters and the materials they accompany are ineffective? Perhaps. But it could also mean that your credentials or background are not exactly what employers are seeking.

To rule out the possibility that your cover letters are causing negative reactions, take steps such as the following:

1. **Review any cover letters you produced within the last year.** Compare them to examples in this book. Try not to read them from the viewpoint of the original writer, but instead pretend you are a potential employer reading this material for the first time, and evaluate it carefully. (This is easier after some time has passed; most people can be more objective about material they wrote a week ago or a month ago than they were at the time they completed it.)

2. **Get someone else to review your letters.** Everyone has friends and relatives, some of whom actually know something! Use your own personal connections to get an unbiased opinion of the effectiveness of a couple of your letters. You might try an uncle who routinely hires people, a friend who has a track record in writing and editing, a career counselor or employment specialist who specializes in helping people land jobs, or anyone else in a position to give advice. Just share a letter or two, and ask for suggestions for improvement.

3. **Keep a submission tracking list.** This is simply a list of letters and resumes you have submitted to various potential employers. Review it periodically and look at any trends that emerge.

KEEP LETTERS ON FILE

Once you have written a cover letter or an electronic equivalent, *do not get rid of it*. "Hard copies" can be useful; copies stored on computer hard drives (or on removable storage devices) are even better. That way, you can use the same basic letter as a starting point for future efforts.

Ideally, you will want to keep a copy of each version that differs in any significant way. Then whenever a new job opportunity arises, you can choose from a bank of letters you have stored on your computer or otherwise maintained on file. You simply change a few details, and then add a point or two to individualize the letter for this specific employer. In almost no time at all, you will have a brand-new version, ready for submission.

Submission Tracking List

Use this list to keep track of the cover letters and resumes you send to potential employers. (For those submittted by e-mail, creat a special e-mail folder and keep an electonic copy of each submission there).

Employer	Date Sent	Response	Comments

MAKING THE MOST OF COVER LETTERS

By now you should have a good idea of the importance of slam dunk cover letters. Even better, perhaps you've thought of some ways to make your own cover letters work more to your advantage in the job application process.

So as you start pounding that keyboard, good luck! Here's wishing you all the best in composing effective cover letters. Be sure to use these letters to highlight your own particular strengths, or to explain something of interest to an employer about your past experience, future goals, or existing potential.

Here are some parting thoughts about cover letters and your efforts to make the most of them.

Meet the Challenge

You're unique. Your resumes and cover letters are not. They follow standardized formats (at least to some extent), and application letters submitted by different people have virtually identical purposes. The challenge is to make your letter stand out from others of its type, while at the same time keeping it within the bounds of professionalism as judged by employers.

Make Every Word Count

Word for word, a cover letter might be one of the most important writing efforts you undertake. The average cover letter consists of fewer than 250 words. Each word really counts. Make sure you take the time to choose just the right words to convey your message in the strongest, most articulate way possible.

It's Worth the Effort

A little effort goes a long way. A trite statement? Perhaps, but it's true nonetheless. Once you come up with a slam dunk cover letter, it can help lead to a great new job. What's more, you can take that letter and reuse it as many times as needed. Of course, each version should be individualized to the situation at hand, but it's generally much easier to revise an existing letter than to create an entirely new one.

Success Awaits

You can succeed at this process. It doesn't take a rocket scientist to write a first-rate cover letter (unless you're applying to NASA). Actually, anyone can do it. Just take your time, study samples of effective letters, and be willing to revise your work until it achieves the desired effect. The end result will be a vital step in your career development!

6

More Sample Slam Dunk Cover Letters

Following are more sample letters for your review. Some are Type A (Always Appropriate) and some are Type B (Bold and Brassy). Note that some are presented as e-mail messages rather than traditional letters.

Use these examples to spark ideas for your own letter-writing efforts. Keep in mind that while formats may vary according to the medium (i.e., "snail mail" versus e-mail), the same general concepts still apply.

Angela Parker
3308 E. Layton Avenue
Milwaukee, WI 53220
(414) 555-4840 (voice mail and fax)
parker22@xxx.com

July 5, 20__

Mr. Richard Ho
Human Resources Officer
Douglas Memorial Hospital
2204 Avalon Drive
Madison, WI 53704

Dear Mr. Ho:

As a qualified medical laboratory technician who will soon be relocating to Madison, I would like to apply for any position you may have for laboratory personnel.

A copy of my resume is enclosed. As you will see, I have three years of experience in the field and appropriate educational credentials as well as national certification.

If you would like more information, please contact me. I would appreciate the opportunity to talk with you at your convenience.

Sincerely,

Amanda Parker

Date: October 24, 20__
To: jmcdonald@eastDallasps.tx.us
From: stargazer@xxx.net
Subject: PR Professional Interested in Joining Your Staff

Ms. McDonald:

This is to inquire about possible employment with the East Dallas school district. I am aware of the broad range of public information services provided by your department, and I would be very interested in joining your staff should a position become available. Either part-time or full-time employment would be of interest.

My background includes an internship with the public information department of the South Houston Public School District. In this capacity, I performed various types of editorial and public information tasks. This included writing news releases, feature stories, print ads, and other materials similar to those produced by your office.

A copy of my resume is attached for your review. If you would like to see writing samples or other information, I would be glad to respond promptly. I would also be happy to meet with you in person to discuss possible employment.

Thank you for your consideration. I hope to hear from you soon.

Kristen Dudley
171 Flanagan Street
Houston, TX 77027
(713) 555-5087
stargazer@xxx.net

Carla Smith-Lawson
931 Indiana Avenue
Winston-Salem, NC 27106
(910) 555-1414
csl@xxx.com

June 3, 20__

Mr. Paul Kiminski
ACME Logistical Services
P.O. Box 10361
Raleigh, NC 27605

Dear Mr. Kiminski:

Thank you for talking with me yesterday about the accounting position advertised in last Sunday's edition of *The Raleigh Observer*. I am quite interested in being considered for this position.

A copy of my resume is enclosed for your review. As I noted in our conversation, I have had six years of experience in providing accounting services in a corporate setting.

After studying the description for the position at your company, I believe that my background provides a solid match with your needs. Please let me know if you would like further information. I would be glad to amplify on my qualifications and interests through a personal interview.

If you would like to discuss this matter, please contact me at your convenience. I will look forward to hearing from you.

Sincerely,

Carla Smith-Lawson, CPA
Enclosure: Resume

TYLER S. JEFFRIES

211 Apex Townhomes
4300 Washington Avenue
Monroe, MN 55416
(608) 555-4124
tsjeffries@xxx.com

November 7, 20__

Jolynn Henderson
Associate Director, Corrections
Minnesota Department of Justice
407 Executive Office Building
Minneapolis, MN 55412

Dear Ms. Henderson:

I am submitting this letter as a follow-up to our recent phone conversation. As mentioned in our discussion, I would appreciate being considered for the caseworker position currently being advertised.

As the enclosed resume notes, I have had three years of experience as a parole officer with the Illinois Department of Corrections. During that time, I earned superior performance ratings from my supervisors. I also have appropriate academic credentials.

Now that I have relocated to Minnesota as a result of my wife's new position in Minneapolis, I am interested in similar work here. I will appreciate your reviewing my background relative to your requirements.

If you would like more information, please contact me. I am available for further discussion at your convenience. I look forward to hearing from you.

Sincerely,

Tyler S. Jeffries

Date: May 19, 20___
To: helenchaffin@MTGPubs.com
From: jgordon@xxx.net
Subject: Application for Staff Artist Position

Dear Ms. Chaffin:

Please accept the attached resume and samples of my work (saved in Word) in application for the position of staff artist with MTG Publications. I am responding to the advertisement appearing in the June edition of *Graphic World*.

I am a recent art school graduate with successful experience as an intern and part-time employee in two full-service advertising agencies. I am adept in using a variety of art production techniques. I especially enjoy working with computers and advanced illustration and desktop publishing software.

If you find it convenient, I would appreciate an opportunity to meet with you in person and discuss the position more fully. I would be happy to share some more examples of my work, including information on disc or "hard copies" if desired.

Please contact me if I can provide additional information. I look forward to hearing from you.

Thank you,

Jessica Gordon
P.O. Box 3412
Pittsburgh, PA 15222
(412) 555-0758

P.S. Please note that I plan to be out of town May 24-27. I would be amenable to changing these plans, however, should you desire to meet at that time.

CAROL KOBAYASHI
417 Fairfield Road
Columbia, SC 29203
(803) 555-0678
Fax: (803) 555-9912
E-mail: ckobaya@scnet.com

July 17, 20__

James O. Morgan, Jr.
Director of Human Resources
Thomas Technical Systems
976 Rittman Road
Columbia, SC 29204

Dear Mr. Morgan:

Please accept the enclosed resume in application for the position of Safety Coordinator that was announced July 16.

I believe my extensive background in occupational safety meets or exceeds the qualifications for this position. While serving as a staff member for the South Carolina Department of Public Safety, I developed a variety of workplace safety initiatives and conducted training on key safety issues for more than 1,000 participants. Through my academic background and professional experience, I am well prepared to take on the responsibilities of Safety Coordinator.

If after reviewing my resume you would like additional information, please contact me. I will be available for an interview at your convenience.

Thank you for considering my application.

Sincerely,

Carol Kobayashi

MARIA LARIOS

17 South Briar Lane
Lancaster, PA 17606
(717) 555-1297
mlarios@xxxx.com

April 26, 20__

Ms. Joyce Albertson, Director of Personnel Services
Lancaster Secretarial Services
P.O. Box 4238
Lancaster, PA 17607

Dear Ms. Albertson:

It is my understanding that your company frequently employs secretaries, word processing specialists, administrative assistants, and other clerical and administrative support personnel. I have specialized in such functions while serving on the staff of the Lancaster city government. Although I have enjoyed my service with this agency, I would like to take on the challenge of a new position.

A copy of my resume is enclosed. As you will see on reviewing it, I have a wide range of experience in providing office support services. I can offer outstanding technical skills, excellent communication capabilities, and a strong work ethic.

If you would like additional information, please contact me. I would be glad to meet at your convenience to discuss opportunities for employment with your company.

Thank you for your consideration.

Sincerely,

Maria Larios

CANDICE HOBBS VICARS
220 Paxton Street
Harrisburg, PA 17111
(717) 555-4793
chvacct@xxx.net

March 17, 20__

Mr. Randall Kipps
Vice President for Personnel and Training
American Hospital Corporation
11 Huntington Street
Harrisburg, PA 17113-2330

Dear Mr. Kipps:

I would like to apply for one of the two accounting positions currently being advertised by National Hospital Corporation. Thus I am providing the enclosed resume.

My previous work experience is very similar to the jobs you are advertising. While serving with Gettysburg College as a fiscal technician, I have gained firsthand exposure to a variety of financial processes and procedures. This experience has prepared me well for a wide range of accounting and financial management duties.

I am a highly motivated and dedicated worker. My strengths include excellent quantitative skills, thorough work habits, and strong capabilities in written and oral communication.

The enclosed resume outlines my employment and educational background. If you would like me to complete an application form or provide more information, please contact me. I would be happy to meet with you at your convenience.

Thank you for your consideration.

Sincerely,

Candice Hobbs Vicars

JASON LAPINSKI

404 Orchard Parkway
San Jose, CA 95134-2018
(408) 555-4973
E-mail: jlapj@xxxt.com

Mr. Roger Wagner, Vice President
Western Manufacturing
21 East Grace Street
Houston, TX 77028

September 19, 20__

Dear Mr. Wagner:

I love to spend money. May I spend some of yours? Actually, my passion for purchasing is real, but I never waste money. Instead, I have earned a reputation for wise, efficient purchasing operations.

With this orientation in mind, I'd like to submit the enclosed resume in application for the position of Purchasing Manager recently advertised by your company.

My background in purchasing has provided me with a firm foundation in performing procurement functions and related tasks. I'm highly experienced in following the strict standards required for effective purchasing in today's competitive business environment.

I would appreciate your reviewing the enclosed resume. Please let me know if I can become a part of your company's future. I'll be glad to provide any additional details you might require.

Your consideration is appreciated.

Sincerely yours,

Jason Lapinski

Darcy Rollins

Mr. Tom Marano, Creative Director
Golden Marketing Services
201 S. Elizabeth Street
Chicago, IL 60607
June 25, 20__

Dear Mr. Marano:

Thank you for taking the time to talk with me today. I enjoyed our telephone conversation.

As we discussed, my background as a copywriter could prove a significant asset should I join your staff. I believe I would bring a fresh perspective to your company and could help in your quest to bring even more outstanding quality to your operations.

The enclosed resume provides important details about my background. After you have reviewed it, please let me know if you would like to discuss present or future needs of your company and how I might meet those needs.

Also, please let me know if you would like to see my portfolio or selected samples of my work.

Yours truly,

Darcy Rollins
112 The Towers
77 North Lake Street
Chicago, IL 60605
(312) 555-2725 (home)
(312) 555-4999 (cell)

BRUCE HAMILTON
Box 494, Station B
Fredericton NB
E3B 5A6 Canada
(506) 555-9937
E-mail: thehamiltons003@xxxx.net

January 12, 20__

Ms. Connie Rice, Vice President
Edison, Inc.
711 Patterson Street
Lima, OH 45801

Dear Ms. Rice:

This letter and the enclosed resume are submitted in the event that you may have a position vacancy for an electronics technician.

I have a solid background in maintaining and repairing various types of electronic devices and systems (see resume for details). Over the past nine years, I have proved myself to be a diligent and resourceful worker.

Should a position be open in the near future, I would appreciate the opportunity to apply. I will be relocating to the Lima area next month.

My resume provides basic details regarding my background and experience. If additional details are needed, please contact me.

Thank you for considering my application. I would appreciate hearing from you.

Yours truly,

Bruce Hamilton

To: afox@isi.com
Date: August 6, 200_
From: rrc22@xxx.net
Subject: Resourceful Engineer Available

Good morning, Ms. Fox:

Do you have room on your engineering staff for an experienced, resourceful mechanical engineer? If so, the attached resume might be of interest. In the event that you need to add to your engineering staff, I would be enthusiastic about applying.

As my resume shows, my experience with North American Aerospace, as well as my educational background, have prepared me well to perform a wide variety of research, development, and production-related tasks. I am energetic, highly motivated, and dependable, and I take great pride in providing work of excellent quality.

I would appreciate the opportunity to meet with you in person to discuss your company's needs and how I might meet them. If you would like letters of recommendation or any other details, I would be glad to provide them.

Thank you for your consideration!

Rudy Carroll
112 Mountainview Drive
Portland, OR 97221
(503) 555-3847 (mobile)

Byron P. Lieu
3358 Peachtree Avenue
Chatsworth, GA 30705
(706) 555-3239 (voice mail)
(706) 555-6689 (fax)
pbl99@xxxx.com

October 1, 20__

Dr. Raul Melendez
Dean of Academic Services
Tri-County Community College
5341 Webb Parkway
Lilburn, GA 30247

Dear Dr. Melendez:

Please accept the enclosed resume in application for the position of Director of Institutional Research as announced September 30.

I believe my extensive background in institutional research ideally meets your needs for this position. While employed with the University of Georgia, I have specialized in performing statistical analyses and other duties similar to those listed in your job announcement.

In addition to my work background, I hold a master's degree in statistics and am a former community college student myself. I hold a deep belief in the value of community colleges, and I am excited at the prospect of working in a two-year college environment. An article I wrote for *Educational Research Journal* (December 1996) addresses the strong future I envision for institutional research in community colleges.

Please review the enclosed resume and call me at the number listed above if you would like to schedule an interview or discuss my interest in this position. I will be available at your convenience.

Thank you for your consideration.

Sincerely,

Byron P. Lieu

KATIE KABULSKI
186 Windy Hill Lane
Atlanta, GA 30339
(404) 555-8812 (cell)
katiek@xxxx.net

Robert S. Fleenor, President
The Sampson Corporation
29 East Wayne Avenue
Long Island City, NY 11101

February 17, 20__

Dear Mr. Fleenor:

I understand that your firm is expanding its operations in Europe. As a recent college graduate with a double major in marketing and French, I am well prepared to deal with various tasks related to international trade. Now that my studies have been successfully completed, I would like to offer my services to your company.

Enclosed is a copy of my resume. You will see that along with my academic preparation, I have substantial marketing experience through part-time employment and an internship in France with the Michelin Corporation. My work record in these situations has been exemplary, as my references will attest.

If a position opens within your company, please consider me. I would be available for part-time or full-time employment.

I will be glad to provide additional information by mail or telephone, or to come for an interview if invited.

Thank you for your consideration.

Very truly yours,

Katie Kabulski

DANIEL HARRINGTON

841 Silverside Court
Wilmington, DE 19850
(718) 555-6359
systemguy@xxxx.net

May 12, 20__

Mark C. Browne
Personnel Manager
Industrial Environmental Services
Wilmington, DE 19851

Dear Mr. Browne:

Thank you for talking with me yesterday. I enjoyed our telephone conversation.

As you requested, I am enclosing a copy of my resume. This will provide you with specific details regarding my experience, training, and overall qualifications.

You will note that I have a great deal of experience in computer programming and systems development. My background with United Data has prepared me to work with a wide range of computer software and hardware, with special emphasis on network applications. Over the past three years I have proven to be reliable, conscientious, and innovative in solving problems and developing new systems.

I would appreciate the opportunity to meet with you in person to discuss your company's employment needs in the computer area. Please consider me for any openings that your firm might have.

Thank you again for taking the time to talk with me. I look forward to hearing from you.

Sincerely,

Daniel Harrington

Linda A. Kinzer
401 Dominion Avenue
Glen Allen, VA 23060
(804) 555-2473
kinzer@xxx.net

November 3, 20__

Ralph Laughton, Director
Office of Personnel Services
Virginia Polytechnic Institute and State University
P.O. Box 219
Blacksburg, VA 24061-0219

Dear Mr. Laughton:

I noted in your "Classified Employee Opportunity Listing" that you plan to hire a Fiscal Technician. I would like to apply for this position (Job number 7081D).

A copy of my resume is enclosed. As you will see, I can demonstrate all the requisite skills and training for this position. In addition, my previous experience in a university setting has prepared me well to function with a diverse group of staff and faculty.

I appreciate your consideration and will be glad to provide any additional details you might request. Please let me know if you would like to discuss my interest in this position or schedule an interview. I will be available at your convenience.

Thank you for considering my application.

Sincerely,

Linda A. Kinzer

Diane Perry
4412 Talbott Avenue
King of Prussia, PA 19406
(610) 555-4456
perrys3@xxx.com

April 6, 20__

Thomas Murphy, Site Director
Concordia College, Rankin Center
303 Albertson Boulevard
Rankin, PA 15104

Dear Mr. Murphy:

I would like to apply for the position of Executive Secretary at Concordia's Rankin Center. Dr. Thomas Culp, my former supervisor and a current member of the administrative staff at your main campus, informed me of this opening and suggested that I apply.

A copy of my resume is enclosed. As you will see, I have had substantial secretarial experience within a higher education setting. In addition, my technical skills include a rated word processing speed of 85 words per minute and mastery of a variety of computer software programs.

If you would like additional information about my background, please contact me. I will be happy to provide other details or meet with you at your convenience.

Thank you for your consideration.

Sincerely,

Diane Perry

Enclosure: Resume

Mark Paulson
214 Oakwood Avenue
Somerville, NJ 08876
(908) 555-8972

May 5, 20__

Dr. James Nichols
Vice President for Instruction
Newton Community College
P.O. Box 8008
Somerville, NJ 08876

Dear Dr. Nichols:

I was excited to see the advertisement in the *Somerville News* that Newton Community College is seeking an interpreter for the deaf. Please accept this letter and the enclosed resume as my application for the position.

Upon reviewing my resume, you will see that I have the appropriate training and experience for this position. In addition, I am a community college graduate myself and am quite supportive of the mission and goals of the comprehensive community college. I would enjoy the opportunity to contribute to student success while working in such an environment.

If you need additional details, please contact me. I look forward to the prospect of an interview.

Thank you for your consideration of my application.

Sincerely,

Mark Paulson

Angela Ramirez
169 Old North High Street
Harrisonburg, VA 24801
(540) 555-3887
amr32@xxx.com

July 5, 20__

Roset H. Knell, Executive Director
Putnam County Fine Arts Center
312 Eden Street
Pulaski, VA 24074

Dear Ms. Knell:

As a recent college graduate with a background in the fine arts, I would like to apply for the position of Program Coordinator as recently advertised.

Enclosed is a resume detailing my education and experience. As you will see, my studies at James Madison University focused on art history and arts management. I have worked in the Rockingham Fine Arts Center the past two summers, performing duties very similar to those listed in your job announcement. I also have experience in coordinating programs for children as well as adults.

Please let me know if you would like more information. I will be glad to meet with you in person or provide any additional details you might require.

Thank you for your consideration.

Sincerely,

Angela Ramirez

Joyce Haga
823 Zion Road
Greenville, SC 29611
(864) 555-6522
jheng@xxxx.net

September 26, 20__

Louise R. Mitchell, Vice President
Tapcom, Inc.
2842 Industry Drive
N. Charleston, SC 29418

Dear Ms. Mitchell:

I would like to apply for the position of Project Engineer as advertised in yesterday's edition of the *Greenville News*. A copy of my resume is enclosed.

You will note that I have proven experience in designing and testing telecommunications equipment through my recent internship at Clemson University. I worked under the supervision of Dr. Morris Davis, a frequent consultant for your company. I am sure Dr. Davis can vouch for my technical capabilities as well as my strong work ethic and positive attitude.

Please let me know if you would like to discuss my background or other details related to this position. I will be available at any time to talk by telephone or to come to Charleston for an interview.

Thank you for considering my application.

Sincerely,

Joyce Haga, P.E.

LATOYA ALLEN-SMYTH

P.O. Box 1429
Dalton, GA 30722
(708) 555-1890
las@xxx.com

December 6, 20__

Louise Evans, Vice President
Camden Incorporated
6072 Horseshoe Lane
Naples, FL 33942

Dear Ms. Evans:

I understand from our mutual acquaintance, Angie Carey, that you may have an opening soon in your public relations department. If so, I would be most interested in applying.

I recently received a bachelor's degree from the University of Georgia with a major in journalism and a minor in public relations. This educational background was supplemented by summer work experience in public relations for a major manufacturing company.

My resume (a copy of which is enclosed) provides specific details about my qualifications. If you would like writing samples or other information, please let me know. I'll be glad to meet with you at your convenience should you wish to discuss employment possibilities at your company.

Thanks very much for your consideration.

Sincerely,

Latoya Allen-Smyth

Jose Rodriguez
P.O. Box 9211
Santa Clara, CA 95053
(408) 555-4307
joserod33@xxx.com

April 14, 20__

Amber Smith, Human Resources Coordinator
Baker Editorial and Publishing
1801 Panorama Drive
Bakersfield, CA 93305

Dear Ms. Smith:

I am interested in being considered for the graphic artist position that has recently become open at your company.

The enclosed resume provides an overview of my educational background and work experience. The latter included two years at Dawson Lane Publications, where I produced a variety of graphic materials including substantial experience in Web page design. As I understand it, this is very similar to the experience necessary for the position you have advertised.

If you would like to review samples of my work, please let me know. I will be happy to send photocopies or to bring a portfolio for your perusal. Of course, I am available for an interview at your convenience.

Thank you for your consideration. I will look forward to hearing from you.

Sincerely,

Jose Rodriguez

James R. Dickson
604 Blade Street
Dayton, OH 45401
(513) 555-0448
jameyd@xxx.net

May 22, 20__

Ms. Amy Moon, Director
Columbus Department of Recreation
268 North Hamilton Road
Columbus, OH 43213

Dear Ms. Moon:

I understand that your department may be expanding in the near future. As new positions in recreation become available, I would appreciate the opportunity to apply.

I am including a copy of my resume with this letter. As you will see, I have a great deal of direct experience in athletics as well as a degree in recreation management from the University of Dayton.

Of special note is my experience as a professional baseball player at the minor league level. Although my playing career ended after two years, I learned a great deal about the professional side of athletics. I also have experience as a volunteer youth counselor.

If you'd like to schedule an interview or otherwise discuss my interest in this position, please call me at your convenience. I look forward to hearing from you.

Thanks for your consideration.

Sincerely,

James R. Dickson

Date: October 25, 20___
To: grturner@emco.com
From: eb33@xx.net
Subject: Application for Computer Technician Position

Dear Mr. Turner:

I would like to apply for one of the openings you have recently advertised for computer technicians. As requested in your ad, I am attaching a resume to this message, which includes the names and phone numbers of three references.

I have two solid years of experience as a computer technician, as well as an associate degree in computer systems design and repair. You will find me a task-oriented, thorough worker with outstanding troubleshooting skills.

Please note that I have no geographic preferences among the jobs your ad listed. I would appreciate being considered for any position for which I might qualify, regardless of location.

As you fill technical positions, please consider me. I will be glad to come for an interview if invited, or to provide additional information by mail or telephone.

Thank you for your consideration. I look forward to talking with you.

Sincerely,

Elaine Bryson
943 State Street
Rochester, NY 14650
(716) 555-4608
(716) 555-3301 (cell)

Kevin White
2121 Russell Avenue
Institute, WV 25112
(304) 555-7662
E-mail: kwhite@xxx.com

May 19, 20__

Mr. Larry Kennedy, Vice President
Henderson Electronics
2210 Kanawha Boulevard
Charleston, WV 25143

Dear Mr. Kennedy:

I would like to apply for the marketing position advertised by your company in the May 18 edition of the *Sunday Gazette*. A copy of my resume is enclosed.

As you will see, I have had significant international experience though a yearlong internship in Europe. I call this to your attention because I understand your firm is increasing its international marketing efforts. In combination with my educational background as outlined in my resume, this experience should provide a strong match with the duties of the position.

If you would like additional details, please contact me. I will be happy to meet with you at your convenience.

Thank you for considering my application. I will look forward to hearing from you.

Sincerely,

Kevin White

Encl: Resume

Megan B. Miller

1298 Kincaid Drive, No. 24
Tampa, FL 33604
(813) 555-5638
(813) 555-9934 (mobile)
mbm22@xxx.com

Richard L. Lewis, Director of Operational Support
Florida TeleCom, Inc.
P.O. Box 2302
Tampa, FL 30323

Dear Mr. Lewis:

Thank you for talking with me today. I enjoyed our telephone conversation.

I am enclosing a copy of my resume, as you requested. This will provide you with more details regarding my qualifications.

You will see that I have a great deal of experience in maintaining telephone systems and providing appropriate technical support. I am familiar with a wide range of equipment and software and am a proven self-starter with an excellent work ethic.

I am available to meet with you at your convenience to discuss your company's needs for technical staff, as well as my capabilities for fulfilling those needs. I will certainly appreciate the chance to apply for any appropriate position openings.

Thank you again for talking with me. I look forward to hearing from you.

Sincerely,

Megan B. Miller

MICHAEL P. ANDERSON _____

1223 Cedarwood Drive
Joliet, IL 60435
(815) 555-3856
andersonhome@xxxx.com

February 17, 20__

Ms. Martha Talbott
Director of Personnel
Joliet School District
Joliet, IL 60435

Dear Ms. Talbott:

Have you ever hired someone, only to regret it later when performance never matched up to promise? When you fill the position of Assistant Director of Computing Services as recently advertised, I hope this problem does not develop.

I can offer one foolproof way to guarantee a successful job search: select me for the position. No, this is not idle bragging; it's a promise based on my proven track record in computer programming and computing services. In fact, as the enclosed resume demonstrates, my credentials meet or exceed all of the qualifications for this position. While employed with Joliet College and more recently with IPP Enterprises, I have specialized in performing duties very similar to those listed in your job announcement.

In addition to my professional background, my deep interest in education would be an asset in serving as a member of your staff. I must admit excitement at the prospect of working in an educational environment once again.

Please review the enclosed resume and call me at the number listed above if you would like to discuss my interest in this position or schedule an interview. I will be available at your convenience.

Thank you for your consideration.

Sincerely,

Michael P. Anderson

DON WHITNEY

3422 Lawrence Place
Hyattsville, MD 20781
(301) 555-2946
(301) 555-1174 (cell)

July 23, 20__

Charles Anderson, Director
Hyattsville Department of Social Services
160 Hooper Avenue
Hyattsville, MD 20781

Dear Mr. Anderson:

How would you like to pick up the morning paper and see your agency's name in the headlines because someone had mismanaged funds? I can assure you that if I were your chief auditor, such a scenario would never take place.

Of course, such a crisis is unlikely in any case, for I realize your agency is well managed and that you have adequate accounting procedures in place. But if you would like to assure yourself of the best possible staff work in this vital area, please consider my application for the position advertised in the *Baltimore Sun*.

Enclosed is a copy of my resume. You will see that I have more than ten years of experience in performing a variety of auditing and accounting tasks, the last four in a public agency similar to your own. This experience has prepared me well to take on the responsibility of your chief auditor's position.

If you would like more information about my background and credentials, please let me know. I will be glad to provide additional information by mail or telephone, or to come for an interview at your convenience.

Thank you for your consideration. I look forward to hearing from you.

Very truly yours,

Don Whitney

✤ TED M. THOMASON ✤
2234 Woodbury Court
Richmond, VA 23240
(804) 555-9553
tmth09@xx.com
October 28, 20__

Ms. Allyson Mauck, Vice President
Thuler Manufacturing, Inc.
P.O. Box 8893
Richmond, VA 23241

Dear Ms. Mauck:

If you're interested in hiring a proven, experienced manager, please read on. As you will see when reviewing the enclosed resume, I can offer all the qualifications noted in your recent advertisement for a human resources director.

I am a dependable, creative manager with a strong track record in human resource administration in a corporate setting. As my resume shows, my background includes appropriate experience and training for a wide variety of tasks related to personnel management.

I would be interested in discussing your position opening and how it is consistent with my background and experience. Please let me know if you would like me to provide additional details or meet with you for an interview.

Your consideration is appreciated. I look forward to talking with you.

Sincerely,

Ted Thomason

Liz R. Janson

226 Nobb Landing
Laguna Hills, CA 92653
(714) 555-3184
(714) 555-7847 (cell)
E-mail: janliz@xxxx.com

Alice Chang, Human Resources Coordinator
California Department of Natural Resources, Region 6
1074 Marauder Street
Chico, CA 95073

Dear Ms. Chang:

I am interested in the position of public information director advertised in Sunday's edition of the *Chico Times*. My resume is enclosed.

As you will see from the information provided, I have extensive experience in public relations and public information activities. I currently hold a position in this area with the California Chamber of Commerce.

I am considering relocating, and your job announcement caught my interest. I believe that my background provides a strong match for the advertised position. In addition, my interest in environmental issues would be an asset in this role.

If you need more information or would like me to submit an application form, please let me know.

Thank you very much for your consideration. I will look forward to hearing from you.

Yours truly,

Liz R. Janson

Appendix A
Helpful Resources

Consult resources such as these in developing resumes and cover letters, as well as in completing other writing projects.

Alred, Gerald and others. *The Business Writer's Handbook.* St. Martin's Press, 2003. Focuses on developing business communications with a personal touch.

Baugh, L. Sue. *Handbook for Business Writing.* NTC Publishing Group, 1994. Covers a variety of business-writing basics, including tips on producing letters and other correspondence.

Cunningham, Helen and Brenda Greene. *The Business Style Handbook: An A-to-Z Guide for Writing on the Job with Tips from Communications Experts at the Fortune 500.* McGraw-Hill, 2002. Offers a wealth of information on business communication, including correspondence.

Hodges, John C. and others. *Harbrace College Handbook.* International Thompson Publishing, 1998. A great desk reference covering rules of grammar, usage, and effective writing with concise, helpful examples.

Provenzano, Steven. *Slam Dunk Resumes.* VGM Career Books, 1994. Offers great insights on developing powerful resumes.

Roget's International Thesaurus. HarperResources, 2001. The standard work of its kind.

Appendix B
Helpful Words and Phrases to Use in Cover Letters

Words/phrases to show *competence*:
    experienced
    knowledgeable
    highly trained
    licensed
    proven
    successful

Words/phrases to show *personal traits*:
    creative
    dedicated
    diligent
    energetic
    enthusiastic

Words/phrases to show *cooperation*:
    appreciative
    at a time convenient to you
    available at your convenience
    glad to provide more information
    grateful
    if convenient
    if you prefer
    please
    thanks
    thank you

Appendix C
Preliminary Worksheet

Fill out this sheet before writing any cover letters. Then use it as a resource in developing application letters.

Your name: _____

Your address: _____

Your telephone number (with area code): _____

Fax number and/or e-mail address, if applicable: _____

Strengths you would bring to any job:

1. _____

2. _____

3. _____

Special factors to mention or explain (for example: recent college graduate, plans to relocate, available for part-time as well as full-time employment, etc.):

1. _____

2. _____

Appendix D
Submission Worksheet

Use this sheet when you have identified a specific job opening. Staple a copy of ad/job announcement here.

Name of company/employer: _____

Position in which you are interested: _____

Type of application (check): _____unsolicited _____job advertised (attach copy of ad)

Application deadline (if applicable): _____

Checklist of required application materials (check all that apply, if known)

_____ resume

_____ letter of application

_____ letters of recommendation

_____ transcripts

_____ certifications

_____ other (list):

_____

How I meet the job requirements: _____

ABOUT THE AUTHOR

Mark Rowh is a professional career counselor and the author of numerous popular career books.

NOTES

NOTES

NOTES

NOTES

NOTES

NOTES

NOTES